Sunset Italian Cook Book

By the Editors of Sunset Books and Sunset Magazine

LANE BOOKS • MENLO PARK, CALIFORNIA

Acknowledgments

The Editors of Lane Magazine and Book Company express especial appreciation to two members of the Italian Government Travel Office who were particularly helpful in the research and development of this book. They are Dr. Luigi Chilleri of San Francisco, California, and Conte Dr. Sigmund Fago Golfarelli of Rome, Italy.

Edited by Jerry Anne DiVecchio

Assistant Editors: Kathryn Arthurs, Judith A. Gaulke

Design: John Flack

Illustrations: Joe Seney

Cover: Spaghetti with Carbonara Sauce, page 33
       Photographed by Glenn Christiansen

Photographers: Glenn M. Christiansen, 38 (all), 73; Richard Dawson, 12; Jerry Anne DiVecchio, Back Cover top right, top center, top left; Darrow M. Watt, 5, 6, 7, 9, 17, 21, 28 (all), 31, 35 (all), 39, 50, 58, 62 (all), 64 (all), 70 (all), 71 (all), 77 (all), 78 (all), 90 (all); Craig Zwicky, 82.

Executive Editor, Sunset Books: David E. Clark

Contents

Special Features:

An Introduction to Italian Cuisine

The Italians know how to eat well; this should surprise no one as they have been masters of the table for centuries. Ancient Romans recorded in detail gustatory extravagances unequalled since their time. The Medici family of renaissance Florence is credited with carrying the Italian kitchen to France and setting the French on their gourmet uprising. Today the influence of Italian foods is felt in cuisines around the world; but perhaps nowhere as naturally as in the American home.

Italians immigrating to this country brought with them a style of cooking that in many cases has become so totally embraced, its foreign heritage would be forgotten if the Italian names did not cling—spaghetti, ravioli, pizza, minestrone, scallopini. Looking back, the relationship between Italy and the New World gains even greater significance. For the Americas gifted Italy with tomatoes for the brilliant red sauces, beans for thick minestrone, corn for polenta, such other foods as turkey, potatoes, and peppers.

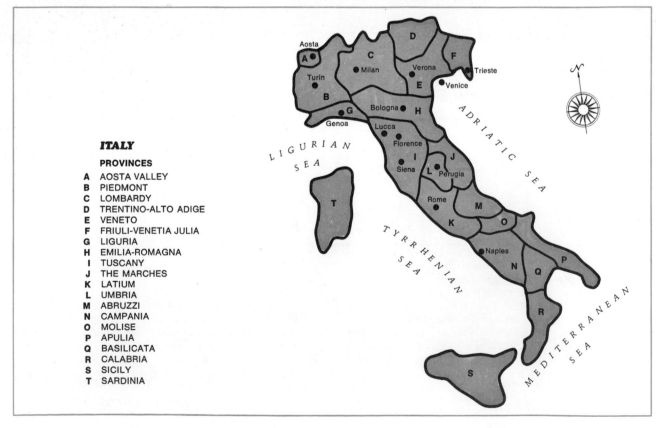

ITALY

PROVINCES

A AOSTA VALLEY
B PIEDMONT
C LOMBARDY
D TRENTINO-ALTO ADIGE
E VENETO
F FRIULI-VENETIA JULIA
G LIGURIA
H EMILIA-ROMAGNA
I TUSCANY
J THE MARCHES
K LATIUM
L UMBRIA
M ABRUZZI
N CAMPANIA
O MOLISE
P APULIA
Q BASILICATA
R CALABRIA
S SICILY
T SARDINIA

Sunset's claim to an understanding of Italian foods reaches back beyond four decades when we began testing and publishing recipes. Italian-American cooks have supplied us with many fine family recipes. Additional enrichments came from readers and our own editors who shared discoveries from visits to Italy.

When we decided to bring the best of these expe-

Cooking Tools and Utensils

1. *Coffee roaster; for a fresh daily supply of coffee beans roasted for espresso, pour beans into cavity. Place roaster on direct heat; rotate handle to toast beans evenly until they are a dark, almost black-brown with a shiny oily film. Grind beans finely to use.*

2. *Espresso style coffee maker with steam jet; fill body of maker with water and set on direct heat. Pressure forces water up through the top and down through removable jacket filled with ground and roasted espresso coffee into the serving pitcher. Steam can also be released through a separate jet; use the steam to heat cups of milk to a steamy froth and blend equally with the espresso to make cappuccino.*

3. *Pasta or noodle machine; hand powered. The pasta dough is shaped by passing between rollers that can be adjusted, and cut by running through the cutting wheels; see pages 27–28.*

4. *Waist-joined espresso maker; heat forces water in base up through coffee into top section. Comes in several sizes.*

5. *Cialde cooky iron; place batter in preheated iron and bake on direct heat (page 92). One of several Italian style cooky irons, each designed for a specific cooky such as the cialde or pizelle (page 93), but all may be used interchangeably.*

6. *Neapolitan macchinetta; water heats in lower section. When boiling, pot is inverted and water drips through center section containing ground espresso into serving unit; remove the top portion and cover server with lid. Comes in a range of sizes.*

7. *Electric espresso coffee machine with steam jet; of a larger scale than the maker above it (2) and capable of producing espresso and steam-heating other liquids in greater quantity. Long lever releases steam that is forced through unit containing the coffee grounds.*

riences together in a cook book, another pilgrimage to Italy was in order. Traveling the length and breadth of the narrow boot-shaped peninsula brought our impressions of Italy up to date, filled in gaps, focused our thinking, and confirmed the validity of the material we had on hand.

Italy Today

We found that regional differences are still distinct despite the growing mobility of the people. Each region treasures dishes, foods, or a philosophy of cooking that makes it unique.

This book contains a selection of these recipes that are most likely to be enjoyed by Americans and duplicated in American kitchens. When we have pinpointed the city or region from which a dish comes; you can locate it on the map on page 4.

All recipes have been thoroughly tested in Sunset's kitchens.

A Regard for the Food

One of the most impressive qualities in the Italian approach to food is the regard for the food itself. A ripe melon is savored for what it is; a piece of meat is seasoned with the intent to enhance but never disguise its basic goodness. A dish as simple as a few slices of pink prosciutto with perfectly ripe figs may be given as much praise as a complex and delicious pasta dish that must be assembled in four or five stages. This book attempts to reflect this honest appreciation for good eating—and to make such standards as easily achieved as possible.

Tools of Showmanship

An Italian cook is half showman, and it's often the tool that gives the performance the proper flair or

Cooking Tools

1. Heavy wooden mallet; does an excellent job pounding veal and other meats thinly, evenly for special dishes (page 43).
2. Spaghetti spoon; one of several inventions—some more effective than others—for lifting long strands of hot cooked pasta from boiling liquid.
3. Perforated skimmers; for lifting foods such as ravioli, gnocchi, vegetables, from cooking liquid.
4. Wire skimmer; used in the same way as the perforated skimmer.
5. Soup ladle; long handled and big bowled for easy serving.
6. Mortar and pestle; for crushing and blending foods, herbs, garlic. Many of its functions can be performed by an electric blender but purists prefer the texture achieved by pounding and mashing.
7. Bagna cauda dish; for individual serving. Hot coals slipped into base keep dipping sauce (page 8) in basin hot. An authentic accessory; but a chafing dish works as well.
8. A good sturdy cheese grater; has a drawer to collect the fine gratings of hard cheese.
9. Cannoli tubes; for making the ricotta-filled pastry (page 90).
10. Rolling pin for noodle or pasta dough; long and tapered for rolling evenly large sheets of dough.
11. Ravioli pin; place sheets of dough under and over ravioli filling; roll pin across dough to shape and seal ravioli (pages 37-38).
12. Metal ravioli shaping pan with rolling pin; another device for shaping ravioli (pages 37-38). Pan comes with various sized depressions.
13. Ravioli cutter; sharp rippled edge cuts apart ravioli shaped by the ravioli pin (pages 37-38).
14. Zampone knife; special retractable blade and razor-like edge for preparing pig's foot sausage.
15. Ravioli stamp; another tool for shaping ravioli (pages 37-38).
16. Truffle slicer; screw adjusts blade so fresh or canned white truffles (page 65) can be sliced as thinly as desired.
17. Pizza cutter; sharp edge of wheel cuts hot pizza.
18. Garlic press; peeled garlic cloves forced through perforated opening makes the mashed garlic for recipes that call for minced or mashed garlic.

dramatizes the presentation. The Italian cookware gathered on these pages can, for the most part, do a job easier, quicker, or better, and in a more amusing way than standard alternates.

Menu Planning

If, when cooking Italian style, you would also like to serve in the Italian fashion, let these thoughts guide you—then adapt them any way you like (an Italian certainly would).

The main meal may be mid-day or evening. For special occasions it begins with the antipasti consisting of one or more dishes from which to choose (based on such variety as vegetables, fruits, meat, fish)—in effect a sit-down appetizer course. However, you might like to present these foods in another room before inviting guests to be seated.

and Utensils

A gentle aperitif such as Campari with soda or dry or sweet Vermouth, will likely precede or accompany this stage of the meal.

Next comes soup or a starch dish of pasta or rice served with an appropriate wine.

Following is meat or fish, typically presented with a vegetable; a starch dish often seems appropriate, but an Italian considers this combination an Americanization. Bread is always available.

Next comes salad, leisurely succeeded by cheese or fruit, then perhaps a sweet, and tiny cup of heavily sugared, bitter rich espresso coffee.

A meal to balance the day around such a filling effort would be starkly simply by contrast—soup or a frittata, salad, cheese, and fruit.

Between these extremes you will likely find the kind of meals you want to serve. The recipes in this book provide detailed suggestions on how to fit them into a menu.

Shopping Guide

Shopping for supplies to cook Italian style presents few challenges if you live in a metropolitan area. A large supermarket will provide all you need for most of the recipes, while a good Italian delicatessen can offer the rest. Surprisingly, many foods that you'd expect were only imported, such as prosciutto, a number of cheeses, sausages, and sweets, turn out to be made domestically. For those of you who can't buy frequently called for items like mild Italian pork sausage or crusty bread, we've included directions for making them at home.

So stock your kitchen with such indispensable basics as olive oil, garlic, Parmesan cheese, canned tomatoes, dried pastas, herbs such as basil leaves, oregano leaves, bay leaves, anise seed, and let this cooking tour begin. Ciao.

1. Zabaglione pan; half sphere shape makes for easy mixing and whipping of zabaglione (page 80) and other sauces.
2. Chestnut roaster; pan holds chestnuts for roasting over direct heat—usually an open fire.
3. Polenta pan; deep shape tapers to narrow base and helps to keep thick polenta confined as it boils (page 41).
4. Classically shaped, unglazed Italian ceramic cooker; the top "locks" to the bottom. Used for baking chicken, meats (page 58). Other styles, often in whimsical shapes of animals, may be glazed or unglazed.
5. Colander; any type will do and is a must for draining hot cooked pastas thoroughly and quickly.
6. Genoese copper saucepan; in-curving bottom and top are typical of the handsome cookware made in this region.
7. Pizza pan; wide shallow round pan used for pizza (page 69) or other pastries.
8. Panettone mold; like a cheesecake pan but deeper and taller. The mold is one way to give the panettone (page 76) an authentic look.

First Courses

Antipasti, crostini, vegetable dishes
to begin or complement a meal

The style and spirit of Italian eating makes itself apparent in the varied ways a meal may begin: perhaps a basket of raw vegetables with a pungent dipping sauce, a collection of savory foods classed as an antipasti, soup, salad, or a lavish preparation such as a pasta.

This chapter deals with dishes that are predominantly vegetable in nature, and with foods you can buy already prepared to serve. One of the delights of Italian eating is the freedom each food enjoys. Many of the dishes here qualify as an antipasto offering, but most are equally at home with a simple meat or fish entrée. Cheese, too, demonstrates this flexibility; it belongs at the beginning or end of a meal to eat as is or with fruit, or as an ingredient in any dish throughout.

The easiest way to gather interesting foods for an antipasto arrangement is to visit an Italian delicatessen. There you will find cold meats and foods such as peperoncini, marinated artichokes, olives, antipasto, caponata, and fried sweet peppers.

Bagna Cauda

The ancient custom of eating from the same dish to signify the spirit of good fellowship is probably most beautifully presented in the Italian spectacle of bagna cauda or, as translated from the Piedmontese dialect, hot bath.

It is just plain raw vegetables dipped, *but not cooked*, in a mutually shared bowl of bubbling butter and olive oil, made bold by garlic and anchovies.

People often consume an astonishing quantity of bagna cauda—it's so easy to justify taking your fill of the fresh, crisp vegetables because very little of the rich sauce actually sticks to each morsel.

½ cup (¼ lb.) butter
¼ cup olive oil
4 small cloves garlic, minced or mashed
1 can (2 oz.) flat anchovy fillets, well drained then finely chopped
  Vegetables prepared according to the following directions
  Thinly sliced French bread or sliced crusty rolls

Choose a heatproof container that will be only half filled by the sauce and add butter, oil, garlic, and anchovies. Place over low heat until butter is melted; keep hot over a candle or alcohol flame and keep heat low enough to prevent browning or burning the sauce. Present sauce with an attractively arranged basket of the vegetables and another basket containing the bread. Hold a vegetable piece in your fingers or impale it on a thin wooden skewer and swirl through sauce; hold a slice of bread under the vegetable to catch any drips as you prepare to eat the vegetable. Eventually the bread soaks up enough sauce to become a tasty morsel, too. Makes 8 to 10 servings. (You can double the recipe for 16 to 20 servings or triple it for 24 to 30 servings.)

Bagna Cauda Vegetables:

You'll need about 1 to 2 cups vegetable pieces per person, but you'll have to estimate quantities while vegetables are still whole. Choose a colorful assortment and cut as suggested to keep a right-from-the-garden look. Cover and chill if prepared ahead. Sprinkle with cold water just before serving.

Artichokes: Break off small outer bracts; cut thorny tips from remaining bracts with scissors. Trim stem ends. Keep in acid water (1 tablespoon vinegar to 1 quart water) until ready to serve. To eat, bite off tender base of each bract.

Cabbage: Cut red or white cabbage in half. Cut vertical gashes in each half. Break off chunks to eat.

Carrots: Leave an inch of stem; peel. Gash carrot not quite through in short sections; break apart to eat.

Cauliflower: Cut out core, keeping head whole. Break off flowerets to eat.

Cherry tomatoes: Dip with stems.

Green beans: Snap off ends and remove strings. Leave whole to eat.

Green or red bell peppers: Cut peppers vertically down to the stems in 8 to 12 sections around the seed center. Break to eat.

Mushrooms: Trim stem ends. Eat small mushrooms whole. Cut large ones through cap only into 4 to 6 sections; break to cat.

Radishes: Cut off root ends and all but one or two leaves to hold for dipping.

Turnips: Peel and cut not quite through in thick slices. Break apart to eat.

Zucchini and yellow crookneck squash: Trim ends; cut not quite through in short sections. Break apart to eat.

Stuffed Olives

An easy and attractive appetizer is this combination of black ripe olives and bright red cherry tomatoes.

1 can (7 oz.) jumbo pitted ripe olives, drained
    About 1 can (2 oz. size) flat anchovy fillets
2 tablespoons olive oil
1 clove garlic, minced or mashed
⅓ cup minced parsley
10 or 12 cherry tomatoes, stems removed

Stuff each olive with half of an anchovy fillet. Place olives in a bowl and mix with oil, garlic, and parsley and let stand at least 1 hour, or refrigerate overnight. Bring to room temperature, then stir in cherry tomatoes. Spear with small wooden skewers to eat. Makes 6 to 8 servings.

Just a few cuts prepare these fresh, crisp, raw vegetables for the eye-catching Italian appetizer Bagna Cauda.

Sicilian Antipasto

This is another flavorful way to marinate olives to serve alone or as part of a selection of antipasto dishes. Here you use the Spanish style green olives.

1 cup pimiento-stuffed Spanish style olives
¼ cup capers, drained
1 cup thinly sliced celery
1 small onion, sliced vertically
2 tablespoons diced red or green bell pepper
2 cloves garlic, thinly sliced
¼ cup olive oil
2 tablespoons wine vinegar
½ teaspoon salt
½ teaspoon fennel seed

Blend olives, capers, celery, onion, pepper, garlic, oil, vinegar, salt, and fennel seed; cover and chill overnight or as long as 3 or 4 days. Bring to room temperature to serve. Spoon on dishes to eat with a fork. Makes 6 to 8 servings.

Florentine Crostini

In all the rest of Italy, crostini means any toast or buttered bread presented at the beginning of a meal. But in Florence, crostini is bread spread with this liver pâté. Serve warm, reheated, or cold, as a snack or appetizer. For another delicious variation, float the crostini in bowls of hot broth.

1 large onion, finely chopped
1 stalk celery, finely chopped
1 large carrot, finely chopped
½ cup olive oil
1 pound chicken livers or calf liver (trimmed of tough membrane)
¼ cup butter
1 tablespoon chopped canned anchovy fillets
2 tablespoons finely chopped capers
    Pepper
    Broth or consommé (optional)
    Minced parsley and whole capers
    Thinly sliced French rolls, toast, or crisp crackers
    Butter

Combine onion, celery, and carrot with olive oil in a wide frying pan; cook, stirring, over medium heat for about 15 minutes or until vegetables are quite soft but not browned. Add liver (if calf liver, cut in chunks) and cook over medium heat, stirring,

for about 5 minutes or until firm and slightly pink in the center (cut a gash to test). Stir in the ¼ cup butter until melted, then add chopped anchovy. Whirl mixture (a portion at a time, if necessary) in a blender to make a coarse purée, or mash with a mortar and pestle.

Blend in capers and season to taste with pepper. *To serve freshly made*, present while still warm; to maintain heat, if desired, place on an electric warming tray or in a chafing dish with a hot water jacket.

To reheat, set the spread over simmering water; stir occasionally until warmed.

To serve cold, thin to a spreading consistency by stirring in broth or consommé, a little at a time.

Mound the crostini spread in a small dish and garnish with parsley and whole capers. Spread generously on sliced rolls, toast, or crisp crackers (plain or buttered). Makes about 2½ cups.

Antipasto Platter

The tomato-based cooking sauce that seasons the vegetables and tuna to make this handsome dish can be saved and used to prepare additional vegetables. Also, you can vary the vegetables; other choices are artichoke hearts, tiny onions, and green beans.

1 cup each catsup, tomato-based chile sauce, and water
½ cup each olive oil, tarragon wine vinegar, and lemon juice
1 clove garlic, minced or mashed
2 tablespoons firmly packed brown sugar
1 tablespoon each Worcestershire and prepared horseradish
    Salt to taste
    Dash of cayenne
½ cauliflower
3 medium-sized carrots
2 stalks celery
½ pound small whole mushrooms
1 jar (8 oz.) peperoncini (small pickled Italian style peppers)
2 cans (7 oz. each) solid pack tuna
1 can (2 oz.) rolled anchovies with capers
    Pimiento-stuffed Spanish style olives for garnish
    Parsley

Combine in a large saucepan the catsup, chile sauce, water, oil, vinegar, lemon juice, garlic, brown sugar, Worcestershire, horseradish, salt, and cayenne. Bring to a boil and simmer a few minutes. Cut cauliflower into flowerets, peel carrots and slice in ¼-inch-thick pieces (use a ruffle-edged cutter if you have one), and slice celery diagonally into 1½-inch pieces. Add to the sauce the cauliflowerets, carrots, celery, mushrooms, and pickled peppers; cover and simmer slowly for 20 minutes, or until tender-crisp when pierced with a fork. Drain tuna and add fish taking care to keep pieces as whole as possible; simmer just until heated through. Spoon into divided or individual dishes, keeping each kind of vegetable and the fish separated. Cool and then chill as long as overnight. Garnish with anchovies, sliced olives, and parsley. Makes 10 to 12 appetizer servings.

Caponata

Caponata is a thick piquant mixture based on cooked eggplant; this version comes from Sicily. As a first course or as part of an antipasto presentation, spoon onto crisp lettuce and accompany with sliced crusty bread, plain or buttered, or spread onto crisp crackers. Caponata can also be served with meats like barbecued beef or lamb as a vegetable dish.

½ cup olive oil
2 cups diced celery
1 medium-sized eggplant, cut in
    ¾-inch cubes
1 large onion, chopped
⅓ cup wine vinegar
1 teaspoon sugar
2 large tomatoes, peeled and diced
1 cup water
1 tablespoon capers, drained
¼ cup sliced pimiento-stuffed Spanish style olives
1 can (2¼ oz.) sliced ripe olives, drained
2 tablespoons minced parsley
    Salt to taste

Heat the olive oil in a large frying pan; add the celery and cook, stirring often, until tender. Remove celery from pan with a slotted spoon and set aside.

Add eggplant to the pan and cook over medium heat, stirring, until it is lightly browned and tender enough to mash easily. Add the onion and continue cooking and stirring until the onion is soft, but not browned. Using a slotted spoon, lift the eggplant and onion out of the pan and add to celery.

Add to the pan the vinegar, sugar, tomatoes, and water; cook over medium heat, stirring, for 5 minutes.

Return the celery, eggplant, and onion to the pan. Stir in the capers, olives, and parsley and simmer, uncovered, about 20 minutes longer. Taste and add salt if needed. Remove from heat, cool, and chill, covered, until needed (at least overnight or for as long as a week). Serve at room temperature; remove caponata from the refrigerator about 20 minutes before you plan to present it. Makes 6 to 8 servings.

Giardiniera

The canned pickled vegetables called giardiniera you see in fancy food stores and Italian delicatessens are easy to make at home. Serve them as appetizers or with cold meats; they also make attractive gifts.

12 to 18 small carrots (about ¾ inch at top)
 1 small bunch celery
 2 red or green bell peppers
 1 large (about 2 lbs.) cauliflower
 1 pound pickling or tiny white boiling
    onions, peeled
 1 cup salt
    Cold water
 2 quarts white vinegar
 ¼ cup mustard seed
 2 tablespoons celery seed
 1 small dried hot chile pepper
2½ cups sugar

Peel carrots; cut in half lengthwise and then in 1½-inch-long pieces; measure 4 cups. Remove strings from celery; slice lengthwise and then in 1½-inch-long pieces; measure 3 cups. Remove seeds and stems from peppers and cut in 1-inch-wide strips. Break cauliflower into 1½-inch-thick flowerets and trim stems.

Stir salt in 4 quarts cold water until dissolved. Add measured carrots and celery, peppers, cauliflowerets, and onions. Let stand, covered, in refrigerator for 12 to 18 hours (overnight); then drain, rinse in cold water, and drain again.

Combine in a 6-quart stainless steel or enamel pan the vinegar, mustard seed, celery seed, chile pepper, and sugar; bring to boiling and boil 3 minutes. Add vegetables and boil 10 minutes or until vegetables are almost tender. Keep hot and discard chile.

Have ready 6 hot sterilized pint jars (to sterilize, immerse in boiling water 15 minutes) and scalded self-sealing lids and bands (pour boiling water over them). Remove 1 jar at a time from boiling water; pack with boiling vegetables; run a spatula around inside of jar to release any air bubbles. Stir boiling vinegar to blend seasonings, then pour into jar to fill up to within ½ inch of rim. Wipe rim, put on lid, and screw on band. Repeat until all jars are filled. Cool on a cloth; test seal. Makes 6 pints.

ARTICHOKES

An artichoke is actually a flower bud; matured, it is a magnificent thistle-like bloom. While the bud is tightly closed, the tender-based leaves (or bracts)

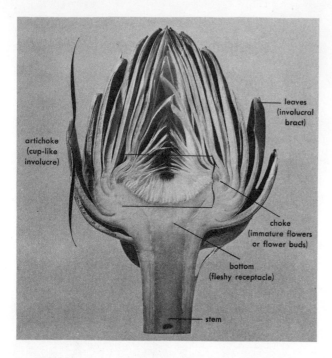

Artichoke in cross section. Edible parts are leaf bases, bottom, stem. Discard choke, fibrous portions of leaves.

How to cook artichokes: You will need a 5-quart kettle for 4 large whole artichokes (4-inch diameter or more before trimming), 6 to 8 medium-sized whole artichokes (2¾ to 3¾-inch diameter before trimming), or about 36 small trimmed artichokes (2½-inch diameter or less before trimming).

In the kettle bring to boiling 4 quarts water with 2 teaspoons salt; add if desired (good for artichokes that are to be eaten whole) 4 to 6 tablespoons vinegar, 3 to 4 tablespoons olive oil, 2 bay leaves, and 10 to 12 whole black peppers.

Rinse artichokes in cool water, then trim according to recipe directions. (If you find a worm hole, trim away his path, making sure the worm is also removed.) Keep in acid water (see left) until all are trimmed; drain.

Add artichokes to boiling liquid and cover; return to a boil and cook until stem end pierces easily with a fork.

Allow 15 to 20 minutes for small artichokes, whole or halved; about 25 to 35 minutes for medium-sized artichokes, whole or halved; and 40 to 50 minutes for large artichokes, whole or halved.

(If you need to cook more artichokes at once, use an additional pan or a larger one, making sure there is enough water to cover artichokes when they are pushed down into the pan.)

Lift from cooking liquid, drain, and serve hot or cold, as desired, or according to the following recipes.

If you want to cook artichokes ahead and reheat them, return the drained artichokes to simmering liquid for 5 to 10 minutes or until heated through.

Roman Artichoke Platter

Diners in Rome are accustomed to the militant look of trimmed artichokes, up-ended with stems in the air, drenched with a light dressing and served as a salad or vegetable.

Choose medium-sized artichokes, allowing 1 or 2 for a serving. Break off outer leaves down to the pale green inner ones. With a knife, slice off about the top third of the leaves (leaves should be trimmed to be completely edible); peel green surface from base and stem, and trim stem end. Cook according to preceding directions.

Drain well and lay gently in a shallow dish in a single layer; pour over enough prepared Italian-style salad dressing to moisten, allowing about 1 cup for 10 to 12 artichokes.

Cover lightly and let stand until they reach room temperature, turning occasionally in dressing. Serve at room temperature, standing artichokes up on cut leaves in a flat platter. Eat with knife and fork, scooping out the fuzzy choke when it is exposed.

overlap on the meaty bottom containing the choke (or immature flowers). The stem is also edible.

In the United States the entire commercial supply comes from the central California coast. They are available fall through winter with the peak season in April and May.

You can eat the whole cooked artichoke leaf by leaf, dipping each bite into a favorite sauce such as melted butter, Hollandaise, or mayonnaise; then scrape off the tender portion from the base of the leaf by pulling the leaf between your teeth. Scoop the fuzzy choke from the center and cut up the artichoke bottom to eat. (In small artichokes the choke is insignificant and you eat it, too.)

Or, before cooking, you can trim the artichoke until it will be completely edible with a fork. This is usually the way small artichokes (also called artichoke hearts) are prepared, and the way they are trimmed and sold as frozen or marinated artichoke hearts.

If you've never cooked a fresh artichoke, be alerted that preliminary handling is important. A cut artichoke darkens when exposed to air and will be more appealing if you preserve its color by immersing at once in an acid water bath (1 tablespoon vinegar mixed with each 1 quart water to cover artichokes).

Carbon steel knives and cast iron and rolled steel (not stainless) cooking pans should be avoided; these metals discolor artichokes and give them a metallic taste.

Savory Artichokes

4 tablespoons olive oil
1 large onion, minced
1 large clove garlic, whole
⅛ pound minced prosciutto, ¼ pound minced baked ham, or 1 stalk celery, minced
2 dozen small artichokes, each about 2½ inches diameter
2 tablespoons minced parsley

In a wide frying pan combine oil, onion, and garlic; cook, stirring occasionally, over moderately low heat until onion is soft; do not brown. Add the meat or celery and cook slowly, stirring occasionally, about 10 minutes longer. Remove from heat; cover.

Cut off top third of each artichoke and break off all tough outer bracts down to the pale green inner ones. Trim stem and split each artichoke vertically. Cook according to directions on page 12. (If you want to prepare this dish ahead to reheat at serving time, immerse hot artichokes in cold tap or ice water; when cool, drain, cover, and chill.)

When ready to serve, add parsley to onion mixture and, stirring, bring to simmer over moderate heat. Add 4 tablespoons water and artichokes and continue to cook, stirring gently, until artichokes are hot and seasonings are blended. Salt to taste, and discard garlic, if desired. Makes 8 servings.

Carciofi Umidi

Basil is exceptionally good with artichokes; you can serve them as a vegetable dish or a first course.

16 small artichokes, 2½-inch diameter or less
   Acid water (1 tablespoon vinegar to each 1 quart water)
2 tablespoons olive oil
1 large onion, chopped
2 medium-sized tomatoes, peeled and coarsely chopped
1 clove garlic, minced or mashed
½ teaspoon basil leaves
   Salt and pepper to taste
½ cup water
   Grated or shredded Parmesan cheese

Cut top third from each artichoke, peel off outer leaves down to pale green inner ones, and peel stem; drop immediately into acid water.

Heat oil in a medium-sized frying pan and add onion, tomatoes, garlic, basil, about ¾ teaspoon salt, ¼ teaspoon pepper, water, and thoroughly drained artichokes. Cover and simmer for 15 minutes or until artichokes are easily pierced. Adjust seasoning with salt and pepper, if needed. Sprinkle with Parmesan cheese. Makes 4 servings.

Artichokes Cellini

Two cheeses flavor the golden crust that forms on this delicate artichoke casserole as it bakes; again, this dish is good served with meats or as a hot appetizer.

12 to 16 artichokes, 2½-inch diameter or smaller
   Acid water (1 tablespoon vinegar to each 1 quart water)
   Boiling salted water
1 small package (3 oz.) cream cheese
¼ cup chopped chives, fresh, frozen, or freeze-dried
¼ cup (⅛ lb.) soft butter or margarine
   Salt and pepper
½ cup shredded Parmesan cheese

Cut top third from each artichoke, peel off outer leaves down to pale green inner ones, peel stem, and cut in half lengthwise. Drop immediately into acid water.

Put artichokes in boiling salted water to barely cover; cover pan and cook about 15 minutes or until artichokes are easily pierced. Drain well. Arrange artichokes close together in a single layer in a buttered, shallow baking dish (one you can serve from). Blend cream cheese with chives and butter. Sprinkle artichokes with salt and pepper and dot evenly with cheese mixture, then sprinkle evenly with Parmesan cheese (you can cover and chill dish at this point until ready to heat). Bake in a 375° oven for 20 minutes or until Parmesan cheese is golden. Makes 4 servings.

Artichokes Vinaigrette

A tart, slightly sweet dressing of red and green bits seasons fresh or frozen artichoke hearts as a salad or first course. They are served cool, so can be prepared well ahead.

1 package (8 or 9 oz.) frozen artichoke hearts
    or 12 to 16 small artichokes, 2½-inch
    diameter or less
6 tablespoons olive oil
2 tablespoons red wine vinegar
3 tablespoons minced sweet pickle
1 tablespoon sweet pickle liquid
2 tablespoons each minced parsley and
    canned pimiento

Cook frozen artichokes in boiling salted water as directed on package until tender. Or trim and cook fresh artichokes according to directions in Artichokes Cellini, page 13. Drain and place in a small deep bowl. Pour over them the olive oil and vinegar. Gently mix in the pickle, pickle liquid, parsley, and pimiento. Cover and chill at least 4 hours or overnight. Lift artichokes from marinade and arrange 6 to 8 halves on each individual plate. With a slotted spoon, remove some of the chopped ingredients from marinade and spoon over artichokes. Serves 4.

Fried Artichokes, Roman Style

Resembling withered roses, these artichokes are an intriguing blend of crispy crusty exterior and tender sweet interior. Serve as a separate course, or with simply cooked meats or poultry.

For each serving prepare 1 medium-sized artichoke (2¾ to 3¾-inch diameter) in this manner: Cut stems flush with bottom. Holding a sharp knife parallel to the side of the artichoke cut away the tough outer leaves, leaving only the tender base of the leaves attached to the artichoke bottom. Cut off about ⅓ of the top of the artichoke and the remaining leaf tips. Firmly press top side of artichoke against a flat surface to open leaves. With a spoon, scoop out choke; immerse artichoke in acid water (1 tablespoon vinegar to each 1 quart water) until all are prepared.

In a frying pan heat 1 inch salad oil on medium heat. Shake moisture from artichokes and pat dry. Add artichokes to oil (do not crowd pan) and brown on all sides, then turn artichokes top sides down and press firmly to open leaves and let hot oil reach the interior. Return to upright position, turn heat low, and continue cooking until artichoke base is tender when pierced; about 15 minutes. Drain well and serve hot; season with salt and pepper.

Italian Beans in a Mist

The wide, quick-cooking Italian or Romano green beans would lose their bright color if prepared the Old World way of simmering slowly in this sauce. Here the sauce, seasoned by a little meat or mushrooms—as you like—is prepared first. Then the beans are cooked quickly in a quantity of water and then blended with the sauce just long enough for flavors to meld. If you are going to serve these beans for a party meal, you will likely want to take advantage of the cook-ahead steps; at serving time you simply reheat the dish.

4 tablespoons olive oil
1 large onion, minced
1 large clove garlic, whole
¼ pound minced baked ham or thinly sliced
    mushrooms
1 pound Italian (or Romano) green beans
    Water and salt

In a wide frying pan combine oil, onion, garlic, and ham or mushrooms and cook over moderately low heat until vegetables are soft. Remove mixture from heat; cover.

Remove ends from beans. Bring 2 quarts salted water to boiling over highest heat and add beans, pushing them down. Cook, uncovered, for 3 minutes after boil resumes. (If you want to cook the beans ahead, immediately immerse in cold tap or ice water; then drain when cold, cover, and chill.)

When ready to serve, add 3 tablespoons water to onion mixture and heat until simmering; add green beans and continue to cook, stirring gently, over moderate heat, until hot. Add salt according to taste and discard garlic, if you like. Makes 4 to 6 servings.

Italian Style Broccoli

A simple warm tomato sauce tops hot broccoli.

¼ cup canned tomato sauce
¼ teaspoon oregano leaves
1 tablespoon vinegar
2 tablespoons butter or olive oil
2 pounds hot cooked fresh broccoli (or 2
    packages, 10 oz. each, hot cooked frozen
    broccoli spears)
½ cup grated Parmesan cheese

Heat tomato sauce, oregano, vinegar, and butter until sauce bubbles and butter melts. Pour over the drained broccoli in a serving dish; sprinkle with the cheese. Makes 6 to 8 servings.

Cauliflower Roma

A richly flavored light sauce of vegetables distinguishes this treatment of cauliflower. Both the sauce and the cauliflower can be cooked separately early in the day, then reheated together at serving time.

4 tablespoons olive oil
1 carrot, minced
1 large onion, finely chopped
1 clove garlic, whole
2 mild Italian pork sausages (about ¼ lb.), casing removed and meat crumbled (optional)
1 stalk celery, finely chopped
1 bay leaf
1 tablespoon tomato paste or catsup
1 large cauliflower
  Water and salt

In a wide frying pan combine oil, carrot, onion, garlic, sausage, and cook over moderately low heat until onion is soft but not browned, stirring occasionally. Add the celery, bay, and tomato paste and continue cooking until carrot is soft, stirring occasionally. Cover the mixture and set aside.

Divide cauliflower into large sections, discarding tough leaves. Drop into 2 quarts rapidly boiling, salted water to cover. Cook, uncovered, over highest heat for 6 minutes after boiling resumes; drain. (If you want to cook the cauliflower ahead, immerse at once in ice water; drain when cold, cover, and chill.)

When ready to serve, add 3 tablespoons water to onion mixture and heat until simmering, then add cauliflower and heat through. Salt to taste and discard garlic clove. Makes 4 to 6 servings.

EGGPLANT

With typical Mediterranean respect for vegetables, the Italians do wonderful things with eggplant. They use both the familiar big shiny purple ones, and the smaller, slender varieties known as Italian, French, or Japanese eggplant—depending mostly upon the clientele of the market.

Eggplant Sauté with Basil

Here the eggplant is cooked simply, which brings out its mellow, easy blending flavor; in other chapters you will find it used as part of more complex dishes.

1 small regular eggplant (about 1 lb.) or 3 or 4 Italian (French or Japanese) eggplants
2 tablespoons olive oil or salad oil
½ teaspoon each salt and crushed basil leaves
  Water
  Salt and pepper

Trim stem from eggplant; cut the regular eggplant in 8 lengthwise wedges, or cut each Italian eggplant in half lengthwise.

Pour olive oil into a wide frying pan over medium high heat. Add eggplant and brown nicely on one cut side; takes about 2 minutes. Then turn (onto skins if Italian eggplant) and add the ½ teaspoon salt, basil, and 3 tablespoons water.

Cover pan and cook over medium heat; check at 1 to 2 minute intervals, adding about 2 tablespoons water at a time as it is absorbed. Shake pan or turn pieces as necessary, until completely tender (the flesh should look creamy throughout); total cooking time will be about 12 minutes. Season, if needed, with additional salt and pepper. Serve hot. Makes 3 to 4 servings.

Eggplant Stuffed Peppers

2 large red or green bell peppers
  Boiling water
1 medium-sized regular eggplant (about 1¼ lbs.)
  About ½ cup olive oil
1 clove garlic, minced or mashed
¼ cup Seasoned Crumbs (see recipe page 16)
  Lemon wedges

Cut peppers in half lengthwise and remove stems, seeds, and pith. Immerse in rapidly boiling water to cover and remove when water returns to boil; drain well. Arrange cupped side up in a rimmed baking pan, side by side.

Trim stem from eggplant and discard. Cut eggplant in ¾-inch cubes. Combine with 6 tablespoons of the olive oil and the garlic in a large frying pan. Cook, stirring with a wide spatula, over medium heat until eggplant is lightly browned and moist looking, about 10 minutes.

Divide hot cooked eggplant evenly among the pepper half shells. Sprinkle eggplant evenly with the seasoned crumbs and drizzle with about 2 more tablespoons olive oil.

Bake, uncovered, in a 375° oven for 30 minutes. Cool to room temperature; serve within 6 hours. Accompany with lemon wedges to squeeze over individual servings. Makes 4 servings.

Eggplant Gratin

Vegetables served at room temperature are a novelty to most Americans, but they are popular in Italy, particularly in the summer, for a very good reason. When neither hot nor cold, vegetables display another interesting, complex spectrum of flavors. And, of course, they must be cooked ahead—an advantage when entertaining.

Several examples of this style of presentation are based on baked eggplant topped with a zestfully seasoned, crumb topping; consider the dish either as an antipasto course or entrée accompaniment.

2 small regular eggplants (about 1 lb. each)
    About ¾ cup olive oil
    Seasoned Crumbs (recipe follows)

Trim stems from eggplants and cut crosswise in 1-inch-thick slices. Pour ½ cup of the olive oil in a rimmed 10 by 15-inch baking pan. Turn eggplant slices in oil to coat them, then place side by side in pan. Top each slice with 1 to 2 tablespoons seasoned crumbs, patting firmly in place. Drizzle crumbs with 4 to 5 more tablespoons olive oil to moisten. Bake, uncovered, in a 375° oven for 1½ hours, or until interior is very creamy. Cool to room temperature; serve within about 6 hours. Makes 6 to 8 servings.

Seasoned Crumbs:

Cut end from a 1 pound loaf sour or sweet French bread. Slice and toast enough of the center portion (about ½ loaf) to make 1½ cups coarse crumbs; whirl, covered, in a blender. Mix crumbs with ½ cup minced parsley, ¾ teaspoon salt, 1 clove garlic (minced or mashed), 1 teaspoon crumbled basil leaves, ¼ teaspoon *each* crumbled rosemary leaves and rubbed sage, and 6 tablespoons olive oil. Cover and refrigerate up to 5 days. Makes about 1½ cups.

Eggplant Sauté with Tomatoes

Follow directions for Eggplant Sauté with Basil (page 15) and when eggplant is almost tender after 6 to 8 minutes add no additional water; instead add 1 can (about 14 oz.) pear-shaped, Italian style tomatoes and liquid, 1 teaspoon sugar, and an additional ½ teaspoon basil leaves. Cover and simmer about 2 minutes, then remove lid and increase heat to reduce liquid to the desired consistency. Makes 4 to 5 servings.

Onions, Bittersweet Style

These onions are also served at room temperature and are good as an antipasto dish or as a vegetable with meats.

4 large onions (choose ones with
    well-rounded shape)
1 teaspoon sugar
1 tablespoon vinegar
½ to 1 cup Seasoned Crumbs (see recipe
    at left)
¼ cup olive oil

Peel onions and cut in half crosswise. Set cut side up in a close-fitting baking pan. Blend sugar and vinegar and drizzle evenly over onions. Pat 1 to 2 tablespoons seasoned crumbs onto surface of each onion half. Drizzle evenly with olive oil. Bake, uncovered, in a 375° oven for 45 minutes. Cool to room temperature; serve within 6 hours. Makes 8 servings.

Peas with Pimiento

Fresh shelled peas are the base of this colorful dish; you can cook the peas and the sauce separately early in the day to simplify last minute preparation. If you cannot get fresh peas, use 4 cups thawed frozen tiny or petite peas, heating them only with the sauce.

3 tablespoons olive oil
1 mild Italian pork sausage (about 2 oz.)
    with casing removed and meat crumbled
    or chopped (optional)
1 large onion, minced
1 medium-sized clove garlic, whole
3 tablespoons chopped canned pimiento
4 cups freshly shelled peas (takes about 3 lbs.
    fresh peas)
    Water and salt

Combine the oil, sausage, onion, and garlic in a wide frying pan. Cook slowly, stirring occasionally, over moderately low heat until onion is soft; do not brown. Stir in pimiento, cover; remove from heat.

Bring 1 quart salted water to boiling over highest heat. Pour in peas and cook, uncovered, for about 3 minutes, or until a rolling boil resumes; drain. (If you want to cook peas ahead, immerse them at once in cold tap or ice water; when cool, drain, cover and chill.)

When ready to serve, add 3 tablespoons water to onion mixture and cook, stirring, over high heat until simmering. Add peas and stir until hot. Salt to taste, and discard garlic. Makes 6 to 8 servings.

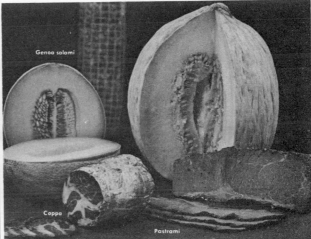

From left: Persian, Honeydew, Cantaloupe, and Casaba melons paired with complementary meats are a classic Italian offering.

Cool Starters-Fruit with Meat

The Italians are masters at presenting fresh fruit with cold meats, achieving a beautiful contrast between the sweet succulence of the fruit and the pungency of the meat.

Classic is the wedge of juicy ripe melon draped with paper thin slivers of salty prosciutto. Less known, but of equal note, are pears and figs teamed with meats. These combinations are elegant openers for most meals.

If you are a traditionalist, you will hold your choice of meats to those that are typically Italian; if you enjoy good eating you will want to explore the additional suggestions that follow.

Melons with Meats

To make each first course serving, place a wedge of seeded melon on a plate and accompany with 2 or 3 thin slices of one of the meats proposed. Eat with a knife and fork.

Other presentations: thin peeled crescents, cubes, or balls of melon rolled up in the meat; a tray to pass with several kinds of melons and several kinds of meats; if portions are generous, you could consider meat and melon as a light entrée for brunch, lunch, or supper.

Crenshaw: Juicy and faintly spicy, this red gold melon is exceptional with baked ham, prosciutto, Westphalian ham, corned beef, pastrami, smoked thuringer, Canadian bacon, galantina, and coppa.

Cantaloupe: An easy going flavor, cantaloupe matches readily with coppa, smoked thuringer, smoked beef, Lebanon bologna, Genoa or dry salami, cacciatore, Westphalian ham, prosciutto, baked ham, Canadian bacon, pastrami, galantina, mortadella, tongue.

Persian: Quite like cantaloupe in flavor, the Persian melon also goes with the same meats (see above).

Casaba: The almost neutral to cucumber-like flavor of the casaba is delightfully refreshing with prosciutto, smoked thuringer, Lebanon bologna, or dry salami.

Honeydew: There's a hint of honey in the white to green flesh of this rich melon, and it is best with highly flavored meats. Prosciutto is its most famous companion; vying for equal billing are coppa, smoked beef, Westphalian ham, Genoa salami, dry salami, or cacciatore.

Figs with Meat

Dark or light fresh figs are superb with dry salami, coppa (especially the hotly seasoned version), and prosciutto. For each first course serving place 1 or 2 figs on a plate with several slices of meat alongside. Eat with knife and fork.

Pears with Meat

In late summer or fall, use buttery textured Bartlett pears in these combinations; during the winter select juicy ripe Anjou, Comice, or Bosc pears.

Pears with prosciutto: For each first course serving place one half of a cored pear (peeled, if desired) on a plate; drizzle with lemon juice to preserve color. Place alongside 3 or 4 paper-thin slices prosciutto, rolled or rippled onto plate. Grind a light sprinkling of black pepper over all. Eat with knife and fork.

Pear fans with pastrami or corned beef: For each first course serving overlap 3 or 4 thin slices pastrami or corned beef on a plate (if corned beef is large, 1 or 2 slices may be adequate). Core ½ peeled pear, then cut in thin slices up to but not through the stem end; fan out fruit as you place it onto the meat. Brush with lemon juice to preserve color. Garnish with a parsley sprig and a lemon wedge to squeeze on to taste. Eat with knife and fork.

Pears with salami: Cut pears in sections with a knife or a coring-wedge cutting tool. Eat fruit out of hand or with knife and fork, accompanying with thick or thin slices of dry salami. Allow ½ pear for a first course serving.

Italian Fried Peppers

Sautéed peppers have a full rich sweetness.

4 large green bell peppers
2 tablespoons olive oil
2 tablespoons butter or margarine
1 clove garlic, minced or mashed
⅛ teaspoon pepper
1 teaspoon oregano leaves
  Salt to taste

Remove stems, seeds, and pith from pepper. Cut lengthwise into strips about 1½ inches wide. Heat olive oil and butter in a large frying pan. Add peppers and garlic. Cook over medium heat until slightly browned, stirring occasionally. Sprinkle with pepper and oregano. Cover and cook over low heat for 15 minutes or just until limp and tender. Salt to taste. Serve hot or warm. Makes 4 to 5 servings.

Italian Roast Potatoes

Slow cooking benefits this onion and potato combination; they bake at meat-roasting temperatures and can go in the same oven with a beef roast.

2 pounds (about 4 medium) baking potatoes
3 large onions, coarsely chopped
½ cup olive oil
1 teaspoon salt
¼ teaspoon pepper

Peel potatoes and cut in ½-inch cubes. Place potatoes and onions in a rimmed 10 by 15-inch baking pan and mix evenly with the oil, salt, and pepper. Bake, uncovered, in a 325° oven for 2 to 2½ hours or until vegetables are a light golden color and the potatoes mash very easily; stir occasionally. Serves 6 to 8.

Parmesan Tomatoes

Serve these tomatoes hot or at room temperature.

3 large firm, ripe tomatoes (about 3-inch diameter)
½ cup Seasoned Crumbs (recipe on page 16)
5 tablespoons olive oil
2 cloves garlic, minced or mashed
1½ teaspoons anchovy paste
1 cup grated Parmesan cheese

Peel tomatoes, trim out cores, and cut each in half crosswise. Gently squeeze out the juice and seeds.

Blend crumbs with 3 tablespoons of the oil, garlic, anchovy paste, and cheese. Divide crumbs among the tomato halves, mounding firmly in place. Set tomato halves, with crumb sides up, in a close-fitting baking pan and pour the 2 tablespoons olive oil into pan. Bake, uncovered, in a 375° oven for 15 minutes. Serve hot or at room temperature; or within 6 hours. Makes 6 servings.

Zucchini, Mediterranean Style

You can cook the sauce and the zucchini early in the day, then reheat them together to serve.

4 tablespoons olive oil
1 large onion, minced
1 medium-sized clove garlic, whole
1 stalk celery, minced or thinly sliced
½ green bell pepper, diced
¼ teaspoon oregano leaves, crumbled
6 small zucchini (about 1 lb.), stem and blossom ends removed
  Water and salt

In a wide frying pan, combine the oil, onion, and garlic; cook, stirring occasionally, over moderately low heat until onion is soft; do not brown.

Add celery, green pepper, and oregano, and cook until vegetables are just tender; stir occasionally. Remove from heat; cover when cool.

Split zucchini lengthwise in halves. Drop into 2 quarts rapidly boiling salted water and cook, uncovered, for 3 minutes after boiling resumes; drain. (If you want to cook the zucchini ahead, immerse in cold tap or ice water; drain when cool; cover and chill.)

When ready to serve, add 3 tablespoons water to onion mixture and cook, stirring, over moderate heat until simmering. Add zucchini and mix gently until heated. Salt to taste and remove garlic, if you wish. Makes 4 to 6 servings.

Soups & Salads

Light and delicate to hale and hearty

Soups and salads are grouped together in this chapter for several reasons. Herein you can find partners for a fine, though simple meal, just as an Italian might; or you can choose a soup or salad to open a meal; or you can select a salad to complement a meat dish, or one that is appropriate to follow the main course.

SOUPS

For everyday living in Italy, the family's main meal often begins with bowls of hot brodo (broth), or the kinds of minestra or zuppa (soup) in this chapter.

The broth may be lightly seasoned and have a little rice, pasta, or bits of vegetables laced through it. Or the soup can be thick and full enough to make a meal. Always present a container of grated or shredded Parmesan cheese to sprinkle into each bowl.

In the following recipes you can use water or canned broth as specified, or use homemade brown stock (recipe follows) for even richer flavor. The stock is also excellent served plain as brodo.

Brown Stock

You can vary this recipe for your convenience by substituting one meat for another—more or less chicken, more or fewer beef bones, pork or ham instead of lamb—or by adding other vegetables such as celery, parsley, leeks, and watercress. The exact quantities of each are less important than the ratio of bulk to water. Some of the meat and vegetables are browned to increase flavor and to add color to the stock.

The freezer can be a great aid in making stock. Store bones and trimmings from various meat purchases until you have enough to work with. Also, you can keep the prepared stock in the freezer.

Here we give directions for clarifying the stock with egg white; if clarity isn't important in the soup you are making, such as a thick bean soup, you can omit this step.

3 **pounds lamb neck, cut in pieces**
4 **or 5 medium-sized onions**
6 **to 8 carrots**
1 **large or 2 small turnips**
2 **teaspoons sugar**
1 **tablespoon vinegar**
6 **quarts water**
1 **teaspoon whole black peppers**
2 **or 3 bay leaves**
3 **pounds bony chicken pieces (necks, backs, wings)**
   About 3 pounds veal shank bones (with a little or lot of meat)
3 **to 4 pounds beef bones (with no meat)**
6 **to 8 egg whites**

In a large kettle (minimum size 12 qts.) thoroughly brown lamb necks over moderately high heat, stirring occasionally. Chop onions, carrots, and turnips and add to pan. Cook over high heat, stirring to free browned particles that stick, until vegetables are very soft and browned.

Push meat and vegetables to one side and set cleared area of pan over most direct heat. Sprinkle onto it the sugar and cook undisturbed until sugar begins to melt and carmalize (take care not to char), then add vinegar and stir well.

Add water, peppers, bay, chicken, veal, and as many of the beef bones as the pot will hold without overflowing. Bring to a boil; reduce heat to very low; simmer, covered, for 4 hours. With a slotted spoon, lift out the bones that protrude up into the fat layer; chill stock. Lift off and discard the solid fat. Heat stock until warm, stirring until melted.

Pour stock slowly through a wire strainer or colander into another large container (at least 8-qt. size). Discard residue.

Return stock to kettle to clarify. Bring to a rolling boil. Beat egg whites until foamy, then whip into boiling stock. Return to a full boil, remove from heat, and let stand until slightly cooled.

Moisten a muslin cloth with cold water, wring dry, and use it to line a wire strainer. Place strainer over a large container. Pour stock through the cloth, a little at a time; egg whites slow the flow. Draw cloth up in a bag and squeeze out as much liquid as possible; discard whites.

For stock of special clarity, repeat clarification process, using another 1 to 2 egg whites for each quart of stock. You should have 5 to 6 quarts of stock; if your yield is less, water can be added now or later to bring the quantity up to as much as 6 quarts.

Cover and chill for as long as 4 to 5 days, or freeze in 1 to 1½-quart containers. For first course servings allow 1 cup stock for each person.

Soup with Rice and Peas

    1 large can (1 lb. 15 oz.) chicken broth
         or 6 cups Brown Stock (see page 19)
    ½ cup short or long grain rice
    1 package (10 oz.) frozen tiny or petite peas
         Shredded Parmesan cheese (optional)

Bring broth to boiling and add rice; cover and simmer 15 minutes. (At this point you can chill soup until serving time.)

Strike the package of peas against a hard surface to separate the peas; add to the boiling broth and simmer gently, uncovered, for 5 minutes. Ladle into bowls; top with cheese if desired. Makes 6 first course servings.

Maritata Soup

There is potential showmanship in the making of this rich, elegant soup. You can complete the last step at the table: have the hot broth with cooked pasta in a chafing dish over direct flame, and add to it the mixture of butter, cheese, and cream that gives the soup its unique, velvety quality.

    6 cups Brown Stock (see page 19) or
         regular strength canned chicken or beef
         broth (or a combination of any of these)
    2 ounces (⅛ of a 1-lb. package) vermicelli
         noodles or ½ cup tiny noodles such as
         pellet or star-shaped egg pastina
    ½ cup (¼ lb.) butter (use sweet butter if you
         use canned broth)
    1 cup freshly grated Parmesan cheese
    4 egg yolks
    1 cup whipping cream
         Salt

Bring broth to boiling. Add noodles; break vermicelli to shorter lengths, if desired. Simmer, uncovered, for 5 to 8 minutes or until noodles are tender to bite.

In a bowl smoothly blend the butter, cheese, and egg yolks, then gradually stir in the cream.

Spoon a small amount of the boiling broth into the creamed mixture, blending; then return all to the soup, stirring constantly. Remove at once from heat. Salt to taste, and ladle into serving bowls. Makes 4 to 6 main dish servings or 8 to 10 first course portions.

Stracciatella

The technique is simple but important in the preparation of this famous scrambled egg soup from Rome.

    4 to 6 cups Brown Stock (see page 19) or
         regular strength canned chicken or beef
         broth
    2 eggs
    ¼ cup shredded Parmesan cheese
    2 tablespoons minced parsley
         Additional shredded Parmesan cheese

Bring stock or broth to boiling. In a small bowl beat eggs to blend with ¼ cup cheese and parsley. Pour mixture into boiling liquid and *immediately* remove from heat; *do not stir.* Ladle into bowls and pass cheese to add to each portion. Makes 4 to 6 first course servings.

Stracciatella: scrambled egg soup. Eggs, cheese, parsley poached in stock. An elegant soup from Ristorante Ranieri in Rome.

Zuppa Pavese

A golden egg yolk floating on a toast raft characterizes this soup.

   Butter
4 slices French or Italian bread
   About ¼ cup freshly grated Parmesan
      cheese
4 cups Brown Stock (see page 19) or 2 cans
      (about 14 oz. size) regular strength
      chicken broth
4 egg yolks

Generously butter one side of each bread slice. Place buttered side up on a baking sheet. Bake in a 350° oven for 15 to 20 minutes or until toasted golden and crusty. Sprinkle each slice with 1 tablespoon of the cheese and broil until cheese is lightly browned.

Meanwhile heat stock or broth to boiling and ladle into 4 soup bowls. Float a slice of the hot toast in each and let stand until edges curl up slightly (2 to 3 minutes). Then carefully slip a raw egg yolk on top of the toast in each bowl. Pass more cheese if desired. Makes 4 first course servings.

Ida's Minestrone

Every region and every cook in Italy has a personal view about minestrone. The word grew out of minestra, and the one thing all minestrones tend to have in common is that they are vegetable soups made with or without meat. The single ingredient most frequently used is dried beans simmered in water or broth to make a bean stock base.

The following minestrones are made in fair quantities, and those using dried beans are good reheated or can be frozen.

This first recipe is typically Tuscan and originated near the old walled town of Lucca. It adapts to the seasons: in fall or winter you might include only carrots, potatoes, onions, and leeks; in spring and summer you could add peas, zucchini, green beans, or other fresh vegetables.

Basic Stock:

1 pound dried pinto, pink, or cranberry
      beans; pick out any foreign materials
      and wash
3½ to 4 quarts water or Brown Stock (see
      page 19)
1 teaspoon salt
10 or 12-inch-long prosciutto bone, or ½
      pound salt pork cut in thick slices
½ cup tomato sauce
¼ teaspoon ground allspice
   Salt and Pepper

Vegetables:

1 cup each of 6 of the following:
   Carrots, cut in small pieces
   Baking potatoes, cut in small pieces
   New potatoes, cut in small pieces
   Curly cabbage, coarsely chopped
   Leeks, coarsely chopped
   Onions, coarsely chopped
   Zucchini, cut in small pieces
   Green beans, cut in small pieces
   Wax beans, cut in small pieces
   Peas, fresh or frozen

Topping:
   Grated or shredded Parmesan cheese

In a large kettle place dried beans, water, salt, and prosciutto bone or salt pork. (You will have to ask a delicatessen to save the prosciutto bone for you—if you use smoked ham or bacon you will find that the smokiness alters the soup's character.) Bring to a boil, cover, and simmer for 3 hours. Drain and save stock. Force half the beans through a sieve (or whirl in a blender with some of the stock). Combine beans, bean purée, stock (including salt pork), tomato sauce, allspice, and additional salt and pepper to taste. Add vegetables, bring to a boil, cover, and simmer 1½ hours. Serve hot. Pass cheese to add to each portion, as desired. Makes 6½ quarts; allow about 1 cup for each first course serving or 2½ cups for each main dish serving.

Minestrone, North Beach Style

This thick minestrone is the kind made by Italian families who settled in the North Beach district of San Francisco.

1 pound dried cranberry or pink beans (pick out any foreign materials, then wash)
4 quarts water (or Brown Stock, page 19)
4 beef marrow bones, each 3 inches long
4 slices meaty beef shanks (each 1 inch thick)
   Cooked vegetables (directions follow)
2 or 3 large potatoes, peeled and diced
½ pound green beans, strings and ends removed and cut in 2-inch lengths
4 small zucchini, sliced
3 cups shredded cabbage
½ cup salad macaroni (ditalini)
   Salt
   Green sauce (recipe follows)
   Grated Parmesan cheese

In a large kettle combine beans with water and bring to a boil. Boil 2 minutes, then remove from heat and let stand, covered, 1 hour.

Add beef bones and shanks and bring to boiling; simmer, covered, for 2 hours. Let cool; remove meat and bones from beans. Mash half the beans by rubbing through a wire strainer; or whirl, a portion at a time, in a blender. Return to whole beans in kettle. Return lean meat to soup; scoop marrow from bones and add to soup; discard bones. Add cooked vegetables to bean stock and bring to boiling; simmer 30 minutes.

Then add potatoes and green beans and simmer, uncovered, for 10 minutes; next add zucchini, cabbage, and macaroni. Simmer, uncovered, 5 minutes more. Season to taste with salt (takes about 2 teaspoons) and stir in the green sauce. Ladle soup into bowls and pass Parmesan to add according to preference. Makes about 6½ quarts soup. Allow about 1 cup for a first course serving or 2½ cups for a main dish serving.

Cooked vegetables: Heat 4 tablespoons olive oil or salad oil in a wide frying pan. Add 2 large onions, diced, and cook until soft. Then add 2 cups *each* diced carrots, celery, and leeks, and cook 5 minutes at simmer. Mix in 1 can (1 lb.) whole tomatoes and liquid, mashing slightly. Simmer rapidly, uncovered, for 10 minutes or until most of the liquid has evaporated.

Green sauce: Sauté ½ cup lightly packed chopped parsley; 1 clove garlic, minced; and 2 tablespoons crumbled basil leaves in 2 tablespoons olive oil until parsley is bright green. Use at once.

Florentine Minestrone

In Florence, the white kidney bean called cannelini is the traditional base of minestrone. This bean is available canned and can be used to make a quickly assembled but flavorful soup. If you are a purist, you will want to add ½ cup uncooked macaroni when you add the green tops of the Swiss chard.

3 cans (15 oz. size) or 2 cans (20 oz. size) white kidney beans and juices
6 cups regular strength chicken broth (or 3 cans about 14 oz. size), or Brown Stock (see page 19)
2 cups water
   Sautéed tomato sauce (directions follow)
1 large onion, finely chopped
2 stalks celery, finely chopped
¼ cup finely chopped parsley
½ teaspoon rosemary leaves, crumbled
1 bunch (½ to 1 lb.) Swiss chard
   Salt
   Grated Parmesan cheese

In a 5-quart or larger kettle combine beans, broth, water, sautéed tomato sauce, onion, celery, parsley, and rosemary. Finely slice the white stems of the chard and add to pan. Bring to a boil and simmer, uncovered, for 10 minutes.

Finely slice the green tops of the chard and stir into soup; simmer, uncovered, for 10 minutes more. Add salt if needed.

Ladle into soup bowls and pass Parmesan cheese to sprinkle over soup. Makes about 5 quarts or 8 to 10 main dish servings.

Sautéed tomato sauce: In 2 tablespoons olive oil, cook 1 large chopped onion and 2 seeded, chopped tomatoes until onion is soft and the liquid has evaporated.

Minestrone, Genoa Style

The story goes that even in the days of Columbus, when Genoese sailors were discovering the outposts of the world, this delicate version of minestrone (and probably one of its most basic forms) was the soup prepared with special care for the wanderers on their return. Herein is captured the sunny, green nature of the Ligurian countryside and the simple comforts of home.

Escarole Soup

Use the tender inside leaves of escarole (also called broad-leaf endive) to make this soup.

1 head escarole
  About ¼ cup shell or elbow macaroni
  Boiling salted water
2 tablespoons butter or margarine
2 tablespoons finely chopped onion
2 cans (about 14 oz. each) regular strength chicken broth or 4 cups Brown Stock (see page 19)
⅛ teaspoon ground nutmeg
¼ teaspoon thyme leaves, crumbled
  Salt and pepper
  Grated Parmesan cheese

Wash the escarole well and discard the coarse outer leaves. Stack the tender green leaves, cut into strips about ¼ inch wide; set aside. Cook macaroni in boiling water until just tender, then drain.

Meanwhile, in a saucepan melt the butter over medium heat. Add onion and escarole, and sauté, stirring, for about 3 minutes. Add the broth, nutmeg, and thyme; bring to boiling. Add cooked macaroni, salt, and pepper to taste. Cook about 1 minute longer. Pass a bowl of the cheese to add to each serving of soup. Makes 4 to 6 first course or luncheon size servings.

It is a soup with the look of summer, and most beautiful served just as it is completed. You can make the stock and pesto sauce ahead, however.

4 quarts water
1 pound each ham and bony chicken parts
¼ pound sliced prosciutto or bacon
2 cups each diced potato and sliced celery
4 small zucchini, sliced in ½-inch pieces
  About 1½ cups sliced leeks
1 pound Italian (Romano) green beans, cut in 2 to 3-inch lengths
½ cup salad macaroni (ditalini)
1 pound peas, shelled
3 to 4 cups shredded white cabbage
  About 2 teaspoons salt
  Pesto sauce (recipe follows, or use 1 cup Pesto Sauce, page 29)

Combine water, ham, chicken, and prosciutto, and bring to boiling. Cover and simmer 2 hours. Strain and reserve stock; discard meat and bones. Bring stock to boiling and add potatoes, cover, and simmer 10 minutes. Remove cover and add celery, zucchini, leeks, green beans, and macaroni and simmer 5 minutes. Stir in peas and cabbage and cook 4 or 5 minutes more. Salt to taste. Ladle soup at once into bowls and spoon in pesto sauce to taste. Makes 6 to 7 quarts or 10 or 12 main dish servings.

Pesto sauce: Combine in a blender ¼ cup chopped parsley, 1 cup lightly packed fresh basil leaves or ¼ cup of the dried herb, and 1 cup freshly grated Parmesan cheese; whirl, adding 6 to 8 tablespoons olive oil, until a smooth thick paste is formed. Or you can mash these ingredients to a smooth paste with a mortar and pestle. Add 2 tablespoons lemon juice. Makes about 1 cup.

SALADS

Italians break salads down into two basic categories: insalata cruda or raw salad, and insalata cotta or cooked salad. Then, when they feel like it, they combine elements of both.

Tender greens with a dressing of a good olive oil made tart with fresh lemon juice or wine vinegar is the most basic salad. Usually it comes as a separate course, but it may also be before, with, or after the entrée.

Elaborations of the green salad are many; you might add slivers of raw vegetables, a few herb leaves (particularly basil), or other refinements such as anchovies or olives.

A selection for insalata cotta would be likely to include cold cooked carrots, zucchini, potatoes, beets, green beans, Swiss chard. Any one of these, or any combination dressed with olive oil, lemon juice or wine vinegar, makes a salad.

Any of the cooked vegetables, combined with any of the raw vegetables, seasoned thusly, makes a salad.

Restaurants often present a colorful salad cart before you with many of these foods and you choose the ingredients for your own salad.

A popular first course called pinzimonio is nothing more than olive oil, vinegar, and salt blended on a small plate, into which you dip bits of crisp vegetables like celery, fennel, raw artichoke leaves, pepper strips, and radishes.

Additionally, the title of salad is tacked onto any number of other cold dishes intended as part of an antipasto offering; saucing can be much more elaborate and often uses mayonnaise.

Antipasto Salad

A New World look at antipasto is the inspiration for this salad-serving concept.

The basic plan is simple. Just arrange a bed of greens in your salad bowl, then top them with a colorful array of a selection of the simpler foods you might find on a tray of antipasti. Bring the salad to the table to show off the colorful arrangement, then mix with an oil and vinegar dressing. The result is a robust salad, appropriate for a first course or adequate as a luncheon entrée to go with hot bread.

The greens: Choose romaine, escarole, red lettuce, butter lettuce, iceberg lettuce, or oakleaf lettuce as the base; add a bit of chicory (curly endive) or dandelion greens for the sharp, bitter tang they contribute. Tear the crisp greens, well washed and drained, into bite-sized pieces and place in a salad bowl (a wide shallow one is more effective for an attractive presentation).

Antipasto toppings: Let your imagination, your sense of flavor and color, and the contents of your kitchen indicate the assortment: canned tuna, drained and broken into chunks; canned anchovy fillets, flat or rolled with capers; Spanish-style, Italian style (or Greek), black ripe, or green ripe olives—whole, chopped, or sliced; hard-cooked eggs, sliced, quartered, or chopped; dry or cooked (Genoa) salami, thinly sliced or slivered; radishes, sliced; green or red bell peppers, chopped or thinly sliced; marinated artichoke hearts, halved or quartered; marinated mushrooms, whole or sliced; Italian style pickled vegetables (giardiniera), whole or chopped; fresh tomatoes, sliced, cut in wedges, or chopped; canned pimiento or sweet roasted red peppers, cut in strips or chopped; green or mild dry onion, thinly sliced or chopped. Arrange the foods of your choice attractively on the salad greens, with each element grouped separately.

The dressing: To blend the hearty flavors of an antipasto salad, a plain oil and vinegar dressing is best. Use 1 part red or white wine vinegar (it may be flavored by herbs or garlic) to 2 to 3 parts olive oil (may be part salad oil). Add dressing, allowing about 1 tablespoon for each cup of greens, to salad; mix to blend and serve at once.

Green Salad with Mint and Bacon

Spinach leaves or tender dandelion greens can be used as substitutes for the romaine in this salad with hot bacon dressing.

1   head romaine, washed, drained, and chilled
½   pound thick sliced bacon, diced
1   large clove garlic, minced or mashed
¼   cup firmly packed, finely chopped mint
2   tablespoons wine vinegar
    Freshly ground black pepper
    Salt

Break lettuce into bite-sized pieces and place in a salad bowl; keep cold. In a wide frying pan cook bacon over moderately low heat until it is just barely crisp; remove with a slotted spoon and drain. To the fat add garlic and cook slowly until soft but not browned. Stir in the mint, the bacon pieces, and vinegar and pour at once over salad greens and mix to serve. Season with pepper and salt to taste and serve at once. Makes 4 to 6 servings.

Sicilian Green Salad

Oranges and olives blend compatibly as salad mates.

1   medium-sized head iceberg lettuce, washed, drained, and chilled
1   can (2¼ oz.) sliced ripe olives
2   oranges, peeled to remove white membrane and thinly sliced crosswise
¼   cup olive oil or salad oil
¼   cup orange juice
2   teaspoons vinegar
1   teaspoon salt
¼   teaspoon paprika

Break lettuce into bite-sized pieces and place in a salad bowl. Top with olives and orange slices. Blend oil, orange juice, vinegar, salt, and paprika; pour over salad and mix to serve. Makes 4 to 6 servings.

Appetizer Salad

Cooked vegetables and a variety of salad greens make this colorful salad.

1 small cauliflower, broken into flowerets
  Boiling salted water
1 head each red lettuce, escarole, and curly
   endive (chicory)
1 can (1 lb. size) each cut green beans, red
   kidney beans, and garbanzos
2 or 3 green onions, chopped (include part
   of the green tops)
6 hard-cooked eggs, sliced
1 cup olive oil
½ cup wine vinegar
  About ½ teaspoon salt
¼ teaspoon pepper
2 medium-sized tomatoes, sliced
1 can (2¼ oz.) sliced ripe olives
1 or 2 cans (2 oz. size) flat anchovy fillets or
   anchovies rolled with capers

Drop cauliflowerets into boiling salted water to cover and boil just until barely tender to pierce. Drain and let cool.

Wash, drain, and crisp greens. Break greens into bite-sized pieces and place in a large salad bowl. Top with the cauliflower, drained beans and garbanzos, onions, and 4 of the eggs. Blend oil, vinegar, ½ teaspoon salt, and pepper and pour over the salad. Garnish top with remaining eggs, tomatoes, olives, and anchovies. Mix and serve at once, adding more salt if needed. Makes 10 to 12 servings.

Insalata di Cipolle

Serve this onion salad with any simple roast of meat or poultry.

6 large mild onions, peeled and thinly sliced
  Water
  Salt
½ cup olive oil
3 to 5 tablespoons wine vinegar
¼ teaspoon oregano leaves
  Freshly ground pepper
¼ cup minced parsley

Cover onions with water and add ½ teaspoon salt. Quickly bring to boiling, uncovered, then drain and cool. Combine with oil, vinegar, oregano, pepper, and salt to taste; chill lightly. To serve, sprinkle with parsley. Makes 6 to 8 servings.

Insalata di Patate e Fagiolini

Cooked potatoes and green beans are a favorite Italian salad; this is like one served in Genoa, which goes well with steaks or hamburgers.

1 pound new (waxy-textured) potatoes
  Water
¼ cup olive oil
1 tablespoon white wine vinegar
  Salt
  Pepper
½ pound green beans, ends and strings
   removed, and cut in 1-inch lengths
2 tablespoons minced onion
  Canned anchovy fillets and capers
   (optional)

Cover potatoes with boiling water and cook just until tender to pierce; drain. When cool enough to touch, peel and dice. Mix with oil, vinegar, and salt and pepper to taste. Set aside to cool.

Cook beans in boiling water to cover, uncovered, just until barely tender; drain and at once immerse in cold water to cool; drain again. Mix beans with potatoes and onions and chill until ready to serve; garnish, if desired, with anchovies and capers. Makes 6 servings.

Spinach Salad
with Pine Nut Dressing

To toast pine nuts or pignoli for this dressing, spread shelled nuts in a single layer in a pan; bake at 350° for 5 minutes or until light gold, shake occasionally.

¾ cup toasted pine nuts, coarsely chopped
½ teaspoon tarragon leaves
¼ teaspoon grated lemon peel
⅛ teaspoon ground nutmeg
½ cup olive oil or salad oil
⅓ cup wine vinegar
½ teaspoon salt
  Spinach leaves or half spinach and half
   butter lettuce
  Ground nutmeg

Blend nuts with tarragon, lemon peel, ⅛ teaspoon nutmeg, oil, vinegar, and salt. Mix well before using. Allow 2 tablespoons dressing for each cup of greens. Sprinkle each salad lightly with nutmeg to serve. Makes about 1⅓ cups dressing.

Pasta

Fettucini, pesto, carbonara, cannelloni, and other marvels

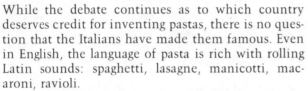

While the debate continues as to which country deserves credit for inventing pastas, there is no question that the Italians have made them famous. Even in English, the language of pasta is rich with rolling Latin sounds: spaghetti, lasagne, manicotti, macaroni, ravioli.

Sorting out the name of a dish from the name of a pasta is impossible as frequently they are one and the same. Here we approach the discovery of pastas from two points of view: those you can buy, and those you must make. A good Italian cook would never hesitate to do both.

Dried pastas, technically, are grouped under the generic term *macaroni* and this includes all shapes and flavors of dried alimentary pastes. They are cooked in liquid and sauced; perhaps with nothing more than a little butter and sprinkling of grated or shredded cheese.

Fresh, filled (often frozen) pastas such as ravioli and tortellini are also cooked in liquid and sauced. They are a big job to make, but occasionally the hours of effort seem worthwhile; however, a good Italian cook would feel free to buy the ready-made product too.

Homemade noodles, another project that requires time and attention, are not especially difficult and are rewardingly delicious; you can make them by hand, but if you have a little hand-powered pasta machine, noodles are easier and more fun to make. As before, you can also buy good freshly made (or frozen) noodles. After boiling, they can be sauced as plainly or richly as you chose.

This chapter is introduced with the making of fresh noodles; following is a collection of sauces suitable for a variety of fresh, dried, or filled pastas. Then we explore some of the multi-step, more elaborate pasta entrées, and related starch-based dishes such as gnocchi, polenta, and risotto.

Homemade Egg Noodles

The velvety texture of homemade egg noodles lifts them well above mere peasant fare. The shaped noodles can be cooked as they are made, or wrapped in clear plastic film and refrigerated up to two days. Or wrap airtight and freeze them up to one month.

    3 egg yolks
    1 whole egg
    2 tablespoons water
    1 teaspoon olive oil
    ½ teaspoon salt
       About 1¾ cups unsifted all-purpose flour

Beat together just until blended the egg yolks, egg, water, oil, and salt. Spoon 1½ cups of the flour into a large mixing bowl and make a cavity in the center. Pour in the egg mixture and stir with a fork until flour is well moistened. Press into a ball.

Sprinkle remaining flour on a board and knead dough until it is very smooth and elastic, about 10 minutes. (Knead the dough just until it holds together and is of uniform texture, if you will be using a pasta machine later, as the squeezing action of the machine is the equivalent of kneading.) Slip dough into a plastic bag and chill 1 hour. Then shape the noodles by hand or use the pasta machine.

To shape noodles by hand: On a floured board, divide dough into 4 equal portions. Roll out 1 portion at a time into a rectangle about 4 inches wide and as thin as possible, about 1/16 inch thick. Cut this into two 10 to 12-inch lengths. Transfer to lightly floured sheets of waxed paper and let sit uncovered while you roll rest of dough. (Drying in the air will prevent the dough from sticking together later.)

Starting at a narrow end, roll up each strip of dough in jelly-roll fashion and cut in ¼-inch-wide strips. Pick up each end of dough and unfurl the coil as you might do a paper serpentine. Lay out on floured sheets of waxed paper and let dry 30 minutes. Makes about 12 ounces (¾ lb.) fresh noodles.

To shape noodles with a pasta machine: Divide dough into 3 equal portions. Working with 1 portion at a time, feed dough through the smooth rollers of the machine, set as far apart as possible. Fold into thirds and repeat 8 to 10 times (this is actually kneading). Whenever the dough appears moist or sticky, lightly flour it.

Set the rollers closer together and feed dough through again. Cut length of dough in half if needed so it is easier to handle. Repeat setting the rollers closer together each time until dough goes through the finest setting. Dough will double and triple in length as it becomes thinner, so cut it in half crosswise whenever necessary for easier handling.

Cut the final strip into 10 to 12-inch lengths. Then feed the dough through the blades of the cutting section. It helps to have another person catch the noodles as they emerge from the machine. (Or you can cut the wide ribbon of dough into rectangles or long ribbons for cannelloni or lasagne—or layer the wide ribbons over and under ravioli filling to make ravioli.) Place on floured waxed paper and let dry 30 minutes. Makes about 12 ounces (¾ lb.) fresh noodles.

To cook homemade egg noodles: Drop noodles into at least 4 quarts rapidly boiling salted water. Return to boiling on high heat and cook, uncovered, for about 2 to 3 minutes or until dough tastes cooked. Pour into a colander and drain quickly. Serve with 6 to 8 tablespoons melted butter and freshly grated Parmesan cheese, or sauce of your choice. Makes about 4 cups cooked noodles.

Fettucini

These first two creamy sauces coat pastas smoothly and elegantly; when used to dress the ribbon shaped fettucini you have a dish very much like the Fettucini Alfredo of Rome. The first sauce is planned for dramatic at-the-table presentation.

6 tablespoons butter or margarine
1½ cups whipping cream
3 to 4 cups hot cooked, drained tagliarini or egg noodles (dried or freshly made)
1 cup shredded Parmesan cheese
    Salt and pepper
    Freshly grated nutmeg (or ground nutmeg)

In a wide frying pan or chafing dish over high heat on a range, melt butter until it is lightly browned. Add ½ cup of the cream and boil rapidly until large shiny bubbles form; stir occasionally. (You can make this part of the sauce earlier in the day, then reheat.)

Reduce heat to medium or place chafing dish over direct flame. Add noodles to the sauce. Toss vigorously with 2 forks, and pour in the cheese and the remaining cream, a little at a time—about three additions. The noodles should be kept moist but not too liquid. Season with salt and pepper and grate nutmeg generously over the noodles (or use about ⅛ teaspoon of the ground spice). Serve immediately. Makes 4 generous or 6 ample first course servings.

Pasta with Sauce Supreme

4 tablespoons butter or margarine
1½ cups whipping cream
½ teaspoon nutmeg, freshly grated if possible
4 cups hot cooked, drained pasta such as fresh egg noodles, fettucini, tagliarini, or hot or cold tortellini, ravioli, or gnocchi
1 egg yolk
¾ cup freshly grated Parmesan cheese
    Grated nutmeg and grated Parmesan cheese

Melt butter with cream and the ½ teaspoon nutmeg in a wide frying pan. Stir in the cooked pasta and bring quickly to boiling; stir gently from time to time. Let boil rapidly 1 to 2 minutes, then blend a little of the hot sauce with the egg yolk.

Remove pan from heat and stir in the egg yolk mixture and the ¾ cup Parmesan cheese, blending thoroughly. Serve at once, offering additional nutmeg and Parmesan cheese. Makes 4 main dish servings or 6 to 8 first course servings.

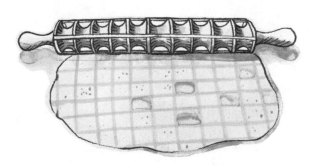

Hand-cranked pasta machine kneads the dough into springy smooth strips before it stretches dough ultra-thin for cutting.

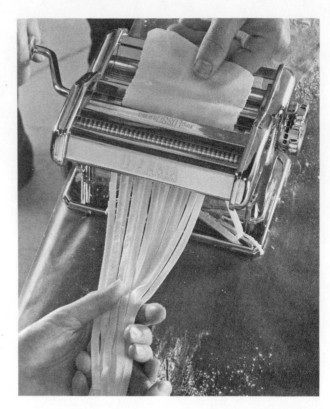

Special cutting attachment on machine makes quick work of dough strip; a few cranks and you have a handful of pasta ribbons.

To cut homemade dough by hand, roll up the dough tightly like a jelly roll, slice it, then grasp the end to unfurl the coil.

Pasta With Peas

Romans make much of this especially delicate preparation unifying green peas, meat-filled pasta, cream, and cheese. This dish is a delightful first course for a meal featuring a simple roast, or it can be the entrée for supper or lunch. Raviolini are miniature ravioli.

- 1 package (12 oz.) freshly made or frozen filled pasta such as tortellini or raviolini, or fresh tagliarini, or fettucini
- 3 to 4 quarts boiling salted water
- 3 cups freshly shelled peas (takes about 3 lbs. peas, shelled) or thawed, frozen petite peas
- 2 tablespoons butter or margarine
- ⅛ teaspoon freshly grated nutmeg
- 1½ to 2 cups whipping cream
- 1 egg, beaten
- 1 cup freshly grated or shredded Parmesan cheese

  Additional grated or shredded Parmesan cheese and grated nutmeg

Drop filled pasta or noodles into rapidly boiling water over high heat; do not cover pan. When water resumes boiling, cook filled pastas 10 minutes or noodles 2 minutes, then add the fresh peas and cook 5 minutes longer; if you use frozen peas, cook only 2 minutes, but allow 15 minutes total for filled pasta and about 7 minutes total for noodles. Drain peas and pasta.

In a wide frying pan melt butter, then add nutmeg and 1½ cups of the cream. Add peas and pasta and quickly bring to a vigorous boil.

Remove pan from heat and stir in the egg evenly; then mix in the 1 cup cheese. If the mixture is a little thick, add more cream to smooth sauce. Sprinkle with more cheese and a little nutmeg. Serve at once. Makes 4 main dish or 6 first course servings.

Basic Pesto Sauce

Pesto alla Genovese or pesto of Genoa is an innocent-looking, quickly made green paste of basil, Parmesan cheese, and olive oil—sometimes with other additions such as pine nuts, garlic, and lemon. It's relatively mild, very easy to like, and a delight when paired with pasta, tomatoes, and a host of other foods. It is also one of the great sauces of Italy.

Basil (sweet basil or basilico) is a popular garden herb, available from spring through fall. Some green grocers offer fresh basil; some will order it for you; or you may have to grow your own.

Pesto also comes prepared: canned pesto is one form; frozen pesto is another. What you make you can also freeze.

2 cups packed fresh basil leaves, washed and
   drained well
1 cup freshly grated Parmesan cheese
½ cup olive oil

Put basil in a blender jar; add cheese and oil and cover. Turning motor on and off, whirl at high speed until a very coarse purée is formed; push pesto down from sides of blender jar frequently with a rubber spatula. Use at once, or cover and refrigerate up to a week, or freeze in small portions. The surface will darken when exposed to air, so stir the pesto before using. Makes about 1⅓ cups.

Pesto butter: Blend 3 tablespoons basic pesto sauce with ½ cup soft butter. Makes ⅔ cup.

Pesto mayonnaise: In a blender jar combine 1 egg, 2 tablespoons lemon juice, and 1 clove garlic. Cover and whirl at high speed until blended. Turn motor off, add ½ cup basic pesto sauce, then turn on high speed and gradually pour in ½ cup melted butter and ¾ cup salad oil. For pouring or dipping consistency, serve sauce at once or at room temperature; for a thicker sauce, cover and chill. Makes 2 cups.

Pesto dressing: Blend 6 tablespoons basic pesto sauce with ⅓ cup wine vinegar, ⅔ cup olive oil, and 1 minced garlic clove. Mix before using. Makes 1⅓ cups.

Pastas and Pesto:

Mixing noodles with the basic pesto sauce, butter, and more cheese is one of the finest pesto traditions; or go one step further and swirl pesto into creamy fettucini.

With pasta: To 4 cups hot, cooked, and drained flat noodles, spaghetti, or similar pasta, add 6 tablespoons basic pesto sauce, 4 tablespoons soft butter, and mix quickly with two forks. Add 1 cup freshly grated Parmesan cheese and mix. Serve with more cheese and pesto to add to taste. Makes 4 to 6 first course servings.

With fettucini: In a wide frying pan, bring 2 cups whipping cream to boil. Blend in 4 cups hot, cooked, drained fettucini noodles (12 oz. uncooked, fresh or homemade) and 6 to 8 tablespoons basic pesto sauce; return to full boil on highest heat. Remove from heat and with two forks mix in 1 cup freshly grated Parmesan cheese. Serve with more cheese and pesto to taste. Makes 6 to 8 first course servings.

Vegetables and Pesto:

All forms of pesto have a special affinity for vegetables.

Add basic pesto sauce to taste to hot, cooked, and buttered artichokes, green beans, Italian green beans, broccoli, carrots, cauliflower, eggplant, potatoes (also baked potatoes), peas, spinach, tomatoes, or zucchini.

Add pesto butter to these same vegetables if they are unbuttered. Spread it also on tomato halves, sprinkle with grated Parmesan cheese, and broil until heated and topping is browned.

Pass pesto mayonnaise to spoon on as desired to any of the vegetables suggested with the basic pesto sauce; or serve mayonnaise as a dip for hot or cold whole artichokes.

Pour pesto dressing as a marinade over cold cooked artichoke hearts, or uncooked and sliced mushrooms, tomatoes, cucumber, or zucchini.

Eggs with Pesto:

Fold about 1 tablespoon basic pesto sauce into a cooked 2 or 3-egg omelet.

Or mash each yolk of a hard-cooked egg with 1 teaspoon *each* basic pesto sauce and mayonnaise, and salt to taste. Fill egg whites with seasoned yolks.

Soups and Pesto:

Add basic pesto sauce or pesto butter, to suit your taste, to individual servings of homemade or canned soup—minestrone, tomato, spinach, chicken, clear broths.

Meat and Fish with Pesto:

Pesto mayonnaise with its touch of lemon is especially suited as the final touch for hot cooked beef, lamb, chicken, lean pork cuts, salmon, Greenland turbot, fillets of sole, and other white fish.

Salad with Pesto:

Pour pesto dressing over salad greens to moisten; for variety include hard-cooked eggs, a few pine nuts, or any of the vegetables suggested above to marinate in the dressing. For seafood salads, pour dressing over cold cooked shrimp or crab.

Meatless Italian Gravy

Meatless gravy (and the meat sauce variation) is excellent with cooked pasta—spaghetti, lasagne, macaroni, ravioli, or tortellini—but it can also be the base of various dishes, each of which is quite distinguished from the other, and you will find reference to this recipe in later chapters.

You prepare this sauce in a fair quantity. Refrigerate it if you plan to use it within eight to ten days; or freeze in recipe size portions. Spoon meatless gravy onto pastas and serve as a first course or to accompany plainly prepared meat or poultry.

1 cup dried Italian mushrooms
   Hot water
3 tablespoons olive oil or salad oil
1 cup packed chopped parsley (about 1 bunch)
2 or 3 stalks celery, chopped
1 medium-sized onion, chopped
2 cloves garlic, minced
   2-inch sprig fresh rosemary or ½ teaspoon dried rosemary leaves
2 small fresh sage leaves or ½ teaspoon crumbled dried sage leaves
4 cans (8 oz. each) tomato sauce
2 cans (1 lb. each) whole tomatoes, chopped, and liquid
1 small dried hot red chile pepper
   About 1½ teaspoons salt

Place mushrooms in a small bowl and barely cover with hot water; set aside. In a large saucepan heat oil and add parsley, celery, onion, garlic, rosemary, and sage. Cook, stirring, until vegetables are soft. Stir in tomato sauce, tomatoes and liquid, and the chile. Pour all but the dregs of the mushroom soaking liquid (the very last may have bits of gritty materials) into the saucepan. Chop mushrooms and add to sauce. Cover and simmer slowly for 3 hours, stirring occasionally. Add salt to taste; serve hot or let sauce cool. Store, covered, in the refrigerator for up to 10 days; or freeze. Makes about 2½ quarts (10 cups) sauce.

Italian meat gravy: Follow directions for the Meatless Italian Gravy, but first brown 2 pounds lean ground beef in the oil, then add vegetables and continue as above. Makes about 3 quarts (12 cups) sauce.

Sauce Julio

This very basic, quickly made tomato sauce is also good with spaghetti; however, you will want to omit the baking step, and simply sprinkle grated Parmesan over the sauced spaghetti and serve.

3 tablespoons olive oil or salad oil
2 cups lightly packed chopped parsley
2 or 3 small garlic cloves, minced
½ teaspoon thyme leaves
¼ teaspoon ground sage
2 cans (8 oz. each) tomato sauce
2 cups water or 1 cup regular strength chicken broth, canned or freshly made, and 1 cup water
2 small dried, hot red chile peppers
   Salt
5 to 6 cups hot cooked and drained tortellini, ravioli, or gnocchi
   Grated Parmesan cheese or thinly sliced teleme or soft jack cheese

In a saucepan over moderate heat combine olive oil, parsley, garlic, thyme, and sage and cook, stirring, until parsley is soft, but still bright green. Stir in the tomato sauce, water, and chiles, and bring to boiling. Simmer gently, uncovered, for about 20 minutes. Salt to taste.

Mix sauce with the hot cooked pasta. Top the dish with a generous portion of the Parmesan and serve. Or place the noodles and sauce in a casserole, cover completely with a layer of the teleme (to prevent pasta from drying), and bake in a 450° oven for 7 to 10 minutes or until cheese melts. Serve at once. Makes about 3 cups sauce, or on pasta, 5 to 6 first course servings.

Fettucce

Gnocchi

Farfalle

Fusilli

Grandine

Ditali

Cresto di Gallo

Tagliatelle all'uovo

Fusilli

Manicotti

Ciocca di Capellini

Conchighe Rigate

Lasagne

Macaroni products come in a wide range of sizes; this demonstrates the variety. Each has several Italian and English names; most relate directly to the shape or intended use of the pasta.

How to Cook Pasta

The secret of cooking macaroni products is to use ample water.

To cook ½ pound (8 oz.) pasta bring to a rapid boil on high heat 3 quarts water with 1 teaspoon salt. Gradually drop pasta (or push long strands in as they become soft enough) into the boiling water until all the pasta is submerged. Cook, uncovered, stirring occasionally and gently until the pasta is tender. To test for doneness bite a piece of the pasta; the color should be even throughout, and texture slightly firm. Cooking times vary with the size and density of the pasta. Very small pasta may cook in 2 minutes; very large shapes may require 15 minutes; the average cooking time is 8 to 10 minutes for pastas like spaghetti. (Be sure to consult package directions for guidance.) Immediately drain the pasta in a colander and serve at once.

To cook 1 pound (16 oz.) pasta follow the preceding directions but increase the amount of cooking water to 4 to 6 quarts and the salt to 2 teaspoons.

Garlic Sauce

Like onions, garlic loses much of its pungency and becomes sweet and mellow if slowly cooked.

½ cup minced garlic (about 1 large head)
¼ cup each olive oil and butter
1 cup minced parsley
   About ½ pound spaghetti, hot, cooked, and drained
   Grated or shredded Parmesan cheese

Cook garlic in butter and oil over medium low heat just until soft but not browned (if scorched, the sauce will be very bitter). Stir in the parsley and cook, stirring, 1 or 2 minutes or until limp but still bright green. Serve hot, or remove from heat and set aside, then gently rewarm to serve. Spoon onto hot cooked spaghetti and top with cheese. Makes 6 to 8 servings as part of the pasta party (see page 40) or 4 first course or side dish servings.

Meatballs in Marinara Sauce

Poaching the moist meatballs in the sauce rather than browning them is the easy technique used here.

¼ pound mild Italian pork sausage
2 cans (about 1 lb. each) marinara sauce
1 cup water
2 pounds lean ground beef
⅓ cup regular strength beef or chicken broth (or water)
1 teaspoon each salt and oregano leaves
1 egg
¼ cup all-purpose flour
½ to ¾ pound spaghetti, hot, cooked, and drained
   Grated or shredded Parmesan cheese

Remove casings from sausage and crumble or chop the meat. Brown meat lightly in a saucepan, then add marinara sauce and the 1 cup water. Heat sauce to simmering.

Meanwhile, mix well the beef, broth, salt, oregano, egg, and flour. Shape beef into balls about 1-inch diameter and drop as they are formed into the simmering sauce; stir gently occasionally to prevent sticking. When all the meat is added to the sauce, continue to simmer for 15 minutes; skim off and discard fat (or chill, lift off fat, and reheat). Serve hot on spaghetti; top with cheese. As part of the pasta party (see page 40) the sauce makes 6 to 8 servings; alone it will make 4 main dish servings.

Salsa Marinara

Shrimp, clams, or scallops season this sauce.

2 cloves garlic, halved
2 tablespoons olive oil or salad oil
1 large can (1 lb. 12 oz.) pear-shaped Italian style tomatoes
⅛ teaspoon seasoned pepper or pepper
½ teaspoon each basil leaves and oregano leaves
   Salt
2 to 3 cups cooked shrimp, clams, or scallops (directions follow)
½ to 1 pound spaghetti, hot, cooked, and drained
½ cup chopped parsley
   Grated Parmesan or Romano cheese

In a heavy frying pan, sauté the garlic in oil until golden; remove and discard garlic. Drain liquid from tomatoes into the pan, crush the tomatoes, and add to pan with the pepper, basil, and oregano. Simmer gently, uncovered, for 30 minutes. Raise heat at end of cooking time to reduce and thicken sauce, if needed. Add salt to taste.

Add the cooked shellfish and parsley to sauce; cook just until heated through, about 5 minutes. Serve over spaghetti and pass the cheese at the table. Makes 4 to 6 main dish servings.

Cooked shrimp: Use about ¾ pound shelled, cooked small shrimp. Or buy about 1 pound medium-sized or large shrimp in shells; cook in simmering, salted water to cover for 5 to 8 minutes, depending on size, until bright pink in color and opaque throughout. Cool, shell, and devein, if needed; then cut into bite-sized pieces.

Cooked clams: Use 2 cans (7½ oz. *each*) minced or chopped clams. Drain juices from clams into pan with the tomatoes (increase heat at end of cooking to reduce and thicken sauce). Add clams and heat.

Cooked scallops: Simmer 1 to 1½ pounds scallops in salted water to barely cover for 7 to 10 minutes or until opaque throughout. Drain and cut each scallop in about 4 pieces; add to sauce and heat.

Tomato Sauce for Pastas

Richly flavored prosciutto flavors this uncomplicated, quick-cooking sauce; if you can not get prosciutto, or simply want to vary the sauce, use in its place twice as much cooked ham.

2 ounces (⅛ lb.) prosciutto, a single piece or sliced
  Olive oil
1 medium-sized onion, chopped
1 large can (1 lb. 12 oz.) pear-shaped Italian style tomatoes
½ teaspoon basil leaves, crumbled
1 teaspoon sugar
⅛ teaspoon fennel seed (optional)
  Salt and pepper
½ to 1 pound spaghetti, hot, cooked, and drained
  About 1 tablespoon chopped parsley
  Grated Parmesan or Romano cheese

Trim fat from prosciutto and dice the meat. In a heavy frying pan cook prosciutto fat over medium heat to render; discard browned fat pieces. If needed add enough olive oil to make 1 tablespoon drippings. Sauté prosciutto and onion in drippings until onion turns golden. Add tomatoes and liquid, basil, sugar, and fennel, if used; break tomatoes into small pieces with a spoon. Simmer, uncovered, for 30 minutes or until thickened.

Season, if needed, with salt and pepper to taste. Serve over hot, cooked spaghetti. Sprinkle with parsley and offer the cheese at the table. Makes about 4 to 6 first course servings.

Carbonara Sauce

Beaten raw egg is the secret of this delicate and delicious sauce; it coats the spaghetti and causes the bits of cheese and meat to cling evenly. It makes a showy offering when assembled at the table.

¼ pound mild Italian pork sausage
¼ pound prosciutto or cooked ham, thinly sliced
  About 4 tablespoons butter
  About ½ pound spaghetti, hot, cooked, drained
½ cup minced parsley
3 well beaten eggs
½ cup freshly grated or shredded Parmesan cheese
  Freshly ground black pepper
  Additional freshly grated or shredded Parmesan cheese

Remove casings from sausages and crumble or chop the meat. Finely chop the prosciutto and combine half of it with the sausage in a wide frying pan with 2 tablespoons of the butter. Cook on medium low heat, stirring, for about 10 minutes or until sausage is lightly browned and prosciutto is frazzled looking. (You can do this ahead and reheat at serving time.)

Blend the remaining half of the prosciutto with the cooked sausage mixture.

If you like, complete the following steps at the table. Have in separate containers the remaining 2 tablespoons butter, parsley, eggs, the ½ cup cheese, and a pepper mill. Add the hot spaghetti to the meats and add butter and parsley. Mix quickly to blend. At once pour in the eggs and continue quickly lifting and mixing the spaghetti to coat well with egg. Sprinkle in the ½ cup cheese and a dash of the pepper; mix again. Serve with more cheese. Makes 6 to 8 first course servings as part of the pasta party (see page 40) or 4 first course servings.

Linguine with Clam Sauce

Clams in their shells garnish the clam sauce for the narrow flat ribbon linguine; the dish makes an intriguing luncheon or supper entrée.

¼ cup each olive oil and butter or margarine
3 tablespoons finely chopped parsley
1 or 2 cloves garlic, minced or mashed
3 medium-sized tomatoes, peeled, seeded, and chopped
¼ teaspoon salt
⅛ teaspoon pepper
  Few drops liquid hot pepper seasoning
¼ teaspoon oregano leaves, crumbled
3 to 4 dozen small hard-shell clams, washed well
2 tablespoons water
  About 6 ounces hot, cooked linguine or spaghetti

Heat the olive oil and butter in a frying pan. Add parsley and garlic and sauté on medium heat for 1 to 2 minutes. Add the tomatoes with salt, pepper, hot pepper seasoning, and oregano. Simmer gently, stirring occasionally, for about 10 minutes; then reduce heat to keep warm.

Meanwhile, put clams and water into a heavy pan. Cover and simmer just until the clams open, 5 to 10 minutes. When cool enough to handle, pluck whole clams from the shells and put into the sauce; save some clams in their shells for garnish, if you wish. Strain the clam juices from the bottom of the pan through a muslin cloth and add juice to the sauce. Reheat and serve over the hot linguine. Makes about 4 main dish servings.

Artichoke Sauce

A variety of vegetables including artichokes are commonly used as the base of interesting sauces for pastas in Italy.

2 tablespoons butter or olive oil
¼ cup minced onion
2 ounces (⅛ lb.) prosciutto or cooked ham, finely chopped
½ cup canned pear-shaped Italian style tomatoes and liquid or sliced baby tomatoes and liquid
1 package (8 or 9 oz.) thawed frozen artichoke hearts, finely chopped
1 tablespoon basil leaves, crumbled
¾ cup whipping cream
¼ teaspoon ground nutmeg
   Salt and pepper
   About ½ pound spaghetti, hot, cooked, and drained
   Grated or shredded Parmesan cheese

Melt butter in a frying pan, add onion and prosciutto and cook, stirring, until onion is soft. Stir in tomatoes, breaking them into small pieces; then add artichokes, basil, and cream. Bring to a boil and cook, stirring, until artichokes are tender and sauce is reduced to about 1¾ cups. Season with nutmeg and salt and pepper to taste. Serve hot, or chill and reheat to serve. Spoon onto hot spaghetti and top with cheese. Makes 6 to 8 servings as part of pasta party (see page 40) or 4 first course or accompaniment servings.

Cannelloni

Well made cannelloni are not achieved without some effort, but the results can be superb. Basically there are four separately prepared elements: the filling, the fresh noodle in which it is enclosed, the cheese that swathes and protects the filled noodle

as it heats, and the sauce. Each can be prepared at least a day ahead, then assembled just before serving.

With a few variations but similar procedure, you can also make a distinguished version of manicotti.

Filling:
4 tablespoons butter or margarine
1 large onion, chopped
1 small clove garlic, whole
¾ pound boned and skinned chicken pieces (dark meat preferred)
½ pound boneless veal
½ pound ricotta cheese
½ cup freshly grated Parmesan cheese
2 egg yolks
¾ teaspoon salt
⅛ teaspoon ground nutmeg

Sauce:
¼ cup (⅛ lb.) butter or margarine
1½ tablespoons all-purpose flour
1 cup milk
1½ cups regular strength chicken broth or Brown Stock (page 19)
1 cup tomato sauce (recipe follows)

Fresh egg noodles:
   Recipe follows

Topping:
   About 1½ pounds teleme cheese

To make the filling, melt butter in a saucepan and cook onion and garlic until soft, but not browned. Cut chicken and veal into approximately 2-inch chunks or cubes, and place in a shallow pan (9 or 10 inches square); add cooked onion mixture. Bake in a 350° oven for 35 minutes. Let cool slightly, add the ricotta, and grind through the finest blade of a food chopper, passing some of the ground mixture through a second time to clear the chopper of solid pieces. Blend thoroughly with the meat mixture the Parmesan cheese, egg yolks, salt, and nutmeg. Cover and chill, as long as 48 hours if necessary.

Prepare the sauce by melting butter in a saucepan; blend in flour and cook, stirring, until golden. Gradually blend in milk and broth. Keep at a very slow boil, stirring occasionally, for about 25 minutes. Add the prepared tomato sauce and simmer at the same rate for about 15 minutes more. Set aside. Reheat when ready to assemble (sauce can be refrigerated several days or frozen).

Shape the cannelloni by mounding about 3 tablespoons of the filling evenly along a 5-inch side of each noodle rectangle; roll to enclose the meat.

To assemble, pour heated sauce about ¼ inch deep into a heat-proof, shallow, rimmed serving container.

Set cannelloni into sauce, leaving at least 1 inch between each. For individual servings of 2 cannelloni each, use oval or rectangular dishes about 4 by 7 inches. For the full 8 servings, use a pan about 16 by 20 inches; however, you can use a combination of pans to make up this area, such as four 8 by 10-inch pans. Top each cannelloni with a slice of teleme cheese just slightly larger in length and width than the top of each noodle. Place in a 425° oven for 10 to 15 minutes or until heated through. Serve cannelloni with surrounding sauce. Makes 8 main dish servings of 2 cannelloni each.

Tomato sauce: Peel 5 medium-sized tomatoes, cut in half, and squeeze out seeds; dice. Heat 1½ tablespoons butter in a saucepan; add 2 tablespoons chopped shallots (or the white part of green onions) and cook until soft. Add tomatoes, ½ cup regular strength chicken broth, ½ teaspoon basil leaves, and ½ teaspoon salt. Simmer uncovered for 40 minutes, stirring occasionally. This sauce freezes. Makes 2 cups.

Fresh egg noodles: Wide fresh egg noodles are the traditional exterior of cannelloni, and if you want to try the dish this way you will likely have to make your own. Today, restaurants more commonly make use of the quickly made thin French pancake.

Pat about 2 cups all-purpose unsifted flour in a firm mound on a board and make a well in the center. In the well, place 6 egg yolks, 1 teaspoon olive oil, and ⅛ teaspoon salt. Using your fingertips, rotating in a tight circular motion, break egg yolks and gradually work flour from edge of the well into the yolks. Add as much flour as eggs will absorb to form a firm dough; they will take up about half of the flour. Sift excess flour and return to container. Knead dough on a lightly floured area of the board until very smooth and elastic, about 10 to 15 minutes; surface of dough should spring back when lightly touched with a finger. Cover; let rest 5 minutes.

Divide dough into 4 equal portions. Roll each portion into a paper-thin rectangle a little larger than 9 by 10 inches. Cut into four 4½ by 5-inch rectangles. Cover until all dough is rolled and cut. If you have a pasta machine, you can work the dough through the smooth roller to achieve the proper dimensions.

Uncooked noodles can be cut and wrapped airtight, each noodle separated by a double thickness of waxed paper. Refrigerate overnight, or freeze. Unwrap and cook.

In a large, shallow pan, bring about ½ inch salted water to boil; add about 1 tablespoon olive oil. Place noodles into the pan without crowding or overlapping. Cook for about 2 minutes or just until tender to the bite, but not soft. With a spatula, lift noodles from water and let drain flat on a cloth. Makes 16 noodles. Use according to directions.

Fill noodles with meat mixture. Spread and mound about 3 tablespoons of filling along wide side of each noodle; roll to enclose.

Cannelloni is still so hot that Teleme cheese topping streams from the noodle filled with veal-chicken mixture.

Manicotti

The same noodles and one of the sauces used for the cannelloni are part of these elegant manicotti.

Filling:

4   tablespoons butter or margarine
1   large onion, chopped
1   small clove garlic, whole
¾   pound boned and skinned chicken pieces (dark meat preferred)
½   pound boneless veal or lean beef
1   cup packed cooked spinach (water squeezed out)
1   cup freshly grated Parmesan cheese
4   egg yolks
1   teaspoon salt
⅛   teaspoon ground nutmeg

Fresh egg noodles:
    See Cannelloni recipe

Topping:
    About 1½ pounds teleme cheese

Sauce:
1   cup tomato sauce (see Cannelloni recipe)
    Supreme sauce (recipe follows)
    Hollandaise sauce (recipe follows)

To make filling, melt the butter in a saucepan and cook the onion and garlic until soft but not browned. Cut the chicken and veal into approximately 2-inch chunks or cubes and place in a shallow pan (9 or 10 inches square); add the cooked onion mixture. Bake in a 350° oven for 35 minutes. Let cool slightly and add the spinach. Grind through the finest blade of a food chopper, passing some of the ground mixture through a second time to clear the chopper of solid pieces. Blend with the meat mixture the Parmesan cheese, egg yolks, salt, and nutmeg. Cover and chill until ready to use (as long as 48 hours if necessary).

Shape the manicotti by mounding about 3 tablespoons of the filling evenly along a 5-inch side of each noodle rectangle; roll to enclose meat. Set manicotti in a buttered, heat-proof, shallow, rimmed serving container, leaving at least 1 inch between each. For individual servings, arrange 2 manicotti in each container, one that measures about 4 by 7 inches; or place altogether on one large tray that is about 16 by 20 inches. Or you can use a combination of pans to make up this area, such as four 8 by 10-inch pans.

Top each manicotti with a slice of teleme to cover top surface completely. Place in a 425° oven for 10 minutes or until cheese is bubbling. Have ready the hot tomato sauce blended with the hot supreme sauce and just before using, stir in the hollandaise (it can be at room temperature). Quickly spoon this sauce all around the manicotti, taking care not to spill sauce on top of them, and return to oven for 5 minutes more. Serve manicotti with surrounding sauce. Makes 8 main dish servings of 2 each.

Supreme sauce: Melt 2 tablespoons butter or margarine in a saucepan, stir in 1 tablespoon all-purpose flour. Gradually blend in ½ cup regular strength chicken broth and ½ cup half-and-half, stirring until thickened. Simmer very slowly for about 8 minutes, stirring occasionally. Beat 2 egg yolks, add a little of the hot sauce, and blend back into saucepan.

Keep warm or reheat over hot water. (You can blend the tomato sauce with the supreme sauce and keep hot or reheat together.) Makes about 1 cup sauce; use all in the preceding recipe.

Hollandaise sauce: Use canned, make your favorite recipe, or prepare this blender hollandaise: whirl 4 egg yolks for about 1 minute in a blender with 1 tablespoon lemon juice, ¼ teaspoon dry mustard, and ¼ teaspoon salt. Melt ¾ cup (⅜ lb.) butter or margarine and slowly pour, in a continuing stream, into whirling yolks until thickened. Chill to store, let stand at room temperature to use. Makes about 1 cup; use all in the preceding recipe.

Salmon Manicotti

Italians are fond of smoked or kippered salmon as a first course, but here it is the base of an unusual variation of manicotti.

½   pound manicotti shells (approximately 8 cylinders, each 5 inches long)
    Boiling salted water
1   pint (2 cups) ricotta cheese
2   egg yolks
2   tablespoons chopped parsley
2   cups flaked kippered salmon
½   teaspoon salt
    Pepper
½   pound teleme cheese
    Tomato sauce (recipe follows)
¼   cup grated Parmesan cheese
½   pound kippered salmon chunks

Cook manicotti in a generous quantity of boiling salted water until tender, about 12 minutes; drain, rinse, and drain again. Mix ricotta cheese well with egg yolks, parsley, flaked salmon, salt, and pepper to taste. Spoon salmon-cheese filling inside cooked pasta cylinders and place side by side on a greased baking dish (about 9 by 13 inches). (You may prefer to use a pastry bag with large plain tip to force the filling into the pasta.)

Slice teleme cheese and arrange to cover the tops of the filled manicotti. Place in a 400° oven for 10 minutes, or until cheese melts and filling is hot. Spoon tomato sauce over manicotti and sprinkle with Parmesan. Garnish with chunks of kippered salmon. Makes 4 to 6 main dish servings.

Tomato sauce: Finely chop 1 large onion and 1 large green pepper and sauté in 3 tablespoons butter or margarine until limp. Add 1 large can (1 lb. 13 oz.) whole tomatoes and liquid and break up the tomatoes with a fork. Pour in 1 cup dry white wine and season with ½ teaspoon salt and dash of pepper. Simmer, uncovered, 20 minutes, or until sauce is reduced and thickened.

Ravioli with Tomato Sauce

Half the fun of making your own ravioli is using the tools designed for the purpose. The speediest way to mass-produce ravioli is with a special wooden pin (see page 38). It marks and seals an entire sheet of neat, puffy pillows at one time. Other techniques and other tools are suggested in the recipe.

You can divide the making of ravioli into easy stages that can be completed well in advance: make the filling and sauce on one day, then make the dough and shape the ravioli the next.

Freshly made ravioli can also be frozen as long as three months. The sauce freezes well, too.

About 4 cups unsifted all-purpose flour
1 **teaspoon salt**
5 **eggs**
2 **tablespoons olive oil or salad oil**
   Meat filling (recipe follows)
   Boiling salted water
   Tomato sauce (recipe follows)
   About 2 cups (5 oz.) freshly grated
     Parmesan cheese

In a large bowl, combine 3½ cups of the flour, salt, eggs, and oil. Stir until ingredients are combined into a stiff ball (there will be some loose particles). Turn out on a board sprinkled with some of the remaining flour. Knead, working in the loose particles, until dough is well blended and pliable, 3 to 5 minutes; add flour as needed to keep dough from sticking.

Form dough into a ball; wrap in a dampened towel and set aside for at least 30 minutes.

An extra long rolling pin is helpful for rolling out the dough. For any of the shaping methods, you first divide the dough in half; then roll out half at a time on a floured board, keeping the remaining dough wrapped in the damp towel. Pull and stretch with your hands as needed to make a very thin sheet of the size specified for each method.

If you use a ravioli pin, roll each half of the dough into a 16 by 22-inch rectangle. Spread the meat filling evenly over one sheet. Carefully pick up and lay remaining sheet of dough on top of filling. With a ravioli pin, roll across top layer of dough, pressing firmly to seal dough layers together to enclose filling. With a pastry wheel, cut filled squares apart along imprinted lines.

If you use a metal shaping pan (see page 6), roll each half of the dough into an 11 by 32-inch rectangle. Then cut each sheet into 8 strips, each about 4 by 11 inches. Sprinkle flour over the pan and shake out excess; lay 1 strip of dough over it (dough will extend over pan sides slightly). Push dough down in the depressions. Fill each depression with meat filling; use about ⅛ of the filling for each pan. (The pans come with depressions of different sizes for large or small ravioli.) Cover with another strip of dough. Pressing firmly, roll pin over top to seal dough and cut ravioli. Invert pan and pull ravioli apart to separate. Repeat with remaining strips and filling.

If you use ravioli stamps (see page 6), roll each half of the dough into a 16 by 22-inch rectangle. With a stamp, lightly mark off one rectangle into as many squares or rounds as possible. Place small mounds of meat filling on each. Cover with the remaining sheet of dough and carefully press the stamp to enclose the mounds of filling, sealing dough layers together, and cutting ravioli apart.

Lift ravioli from board with a spatula. (You can freeze them at this point, if you wish: arrange ravioli in a single layer on a flour dusted cooky sheet; dust tops with flour, cover, and freeze until firm. Then package airtight in plastic bags or rigid containers.)

To cook, drop freshly made or frozen ravioli into boiling, salted water. Return to boil and simmer gently, stirring carefully several times, for 8 to 10 minutes, or until just tender and pasta is translucent clear through; drain well.

To serve, spoon ravioli and tomato sauce into a large rimmed serving dish or onto individual plates. Sprinkle with some of the grated cheese, and pass the balance of the cheese at the table. Makes 8 to 10 generous main dish servings.

Meat filling: In a large frying pan heat 1 tablespoon olive oil over medium heat; add 1 small onion, chopped, and 1 clove garlic, minced or mashed. Sauté until onion is limp, about 5 minutes. Add ½ pound ground pork shoulder, lean ground beef, or ground veal; cook, stirring, until meat is crumbly and brown. Add 1 package (10 oz.) frozen chopped spinach and cook, uncovered, over medium high heat until spinach is thawed and liquid is evaporated.

Remove from heat and stir in ½ cup finely chopped, cooked chicken; ⅛ teaspoon *each* thyme leaves, marjoram leaves, rosemary leaves, and salt; dash pepper; 1 egg; and 2 tablespoons *each* fine dry bread crumbs and freshly grated Parmesan cheese. Mix well and set aside. (Or cover and chill overnight; allow to come to room temperature before using.)

Tomato sauce: Soak 2 packages (½ oz. *each*) dried Italian mushrooms in 1 cup tepid water until pliable,

about 5 minutes. Drain, wash well, and chop; set aside. In a Dutch oven heat 3 tablespoons olive oil over medium heat; add 2 large onions, finely chopped; 2 cloves garlic, minced or mashed; and 2 medium-sized carrots, finely chopped. Sauté 5 minutes.

Stir in the chopped mushrooms; 2 cans (14 oz. *each*) regular strength beef broth; 2 cans (1 lb. 12 oz. *each*) pear-shaped Italian style tomatoes (break up tomatoes with a fork); 1 teaspoon *each* salt, oregano leaves, rosemary leaves, and sugar; 2 tablespoons basil leaves; and ¼ teaspoon pepper. Boil gently, uncovered, for about 1½ hours or until sauce is thickened, stirring occasionally.

One Way to Shape Ravioli

One way to shape ravioli: You start by enclosing the savory meat-and-vegetable filling between two thin sheets of dough.

With a wooden marking pin, roll across sandwichlike structure; press firmly to seal layers together and imprint cutting lines.

Then cut the ravioli apart with a pastry wheel to make fancy fluted edges, following lines made with the marking pin.

Ladle hot, flavorful tomato sauce over perfectly cooked hot, drained ravioli. Top each portion with grated Parmesan cheese.

Potato Gnocchi

Gnocchi are almost easier to make than pronounce (*nyok*-kee). The word means lumps and is descriptive of the shapes and flavors gnocchi assume.

Here, they are tender little potato-based, bow shaped dumplings with a fine veal sauce. Others can be either pasta in a fanciful shape (with or without potato as a base) to boil and sauce, or cooked cereal, cut in pieces, to sauce and bake.

This dough should be used as soon as it is prepared; otherwise it tends to become too soft to handle easily. The cooked gnocchi, however, can be kept warm for several hours before serving and the sauce can be made days ahead.

Shape gnocchi into little bows by forming a rope of the potato dough. Cut rope in short lengths, and roll under your finger.

3 cups mashed potatoes
   (directions follow)
1½ cups unsifted all-purpose flour
1½ teaspoons salt
1 tablespoon olive oil
2 eggs, slightly beaten
   All-purpose flour
   Boiling salted water
2 to 3 tablespoons melted butter or
   margarine
   Veal sauce, heated (recipe follows)
1½ cups shredded Parmesan or dry jack
   cheese or ¾ pound thinly sliced teleme
   cheese

Measure the potatoes into a bowl and add the 1½ cups of flour, the salt, and the oil, and blend with a fork. Add eggs and blend thoroughly into potato mixture. Turn dough out onto a floured board and knead gently about 15 times. Shape into a fat loaf and set on a floured area to prevent sticking.

Cut off one piece of dough at a time (about ½ cup's worth) and roll on a very lightly floured board into a cord ⅜ inch thick. Cut cord in 1¼-inch lengths. Roll each segment in the center lightly under your forefinger to give the piece a bow shape. Set shaped gnocchi aside on a lightly floured pan such as a baking sheet; the pieces should not touch.

When all the dough is shaped, cook the gnocchi by dropping about ⅓ of them at a time into about 3 quarts of boiling salted water. Cook for 5 minutes after they return to surface of water (stir gently if they haven't popped up in about 1 minute). Keep water at a slow boil.

Remove cooked gnocchi from water with a slotted spoon, draining well. Place cooked gnocchi in a shallow rimmed pan (such as a jellyroll pan) and mix gently with the melted butter. Cover tightly with foil and keep in a warm place while you cook the remaining gnocchi.

You can hold the gnocchi in a 150° or lower oven for as long as 3 hours, keeping them well covered to retain moisture. Flavor is best if they don't cool after cooking.

To serve, arrange a layer of about half the gnocchi in a wide, shallow rimmed, oven-proof dish, and top with about half the hot veal sauce and half the cheese. Top with remaining gnocchi, sauce, and cheese. Heat in a 375° oven for about 10 minutes or until cheese melts and gnocchi are piping hot. Broil top lightly if desired. Makes 4 to 6 main dish servings or about 8 first course servings.

Mashed potatoes: You can use dehydrated instant mashed potatoes or fresh potatoes. Cook peeled potatoes until tender in unsalted boiling water and drain thoroughly, then rub through a fine wire strainer. To prepare instant dehydrated mashed potatoes, heat the amount of water called for on package to make 6 to 8 servings; stir in potatoes as directed. Add no seasonings or other ingredients. Measure 3 cups; use at once.

Veal sauce: Combine ½ cup dried Italian mushrooms with 1 cup warm water and let stand at least 30 minutes. Meanwhile, finely mince ¼ cup pork fat or bacon and place in a large frying pan with 3 tablespoons olive oil. Finely chop ¾ pound fat-free boneless veal and add to fat in pan along with 1 medium-sized minced onion, 1 finely diced carrot, and 2 stalks finely chopped celery. Cook over medium heat, stirring, until vegetables are soft.

Drain mushrooms, rinse in water and drain again; add to meat mixture. Also add 1 can (8 oz.) tomato sauce, 1 can (1 lb.) whole tomatoes and liquid (break tomatoes apart in pan), 1 cup dry red wine, 1½ teaspoons salt, ¼ teaspoon ground allspice, and a dash of pepper.

Simmer about 2 hours, uncovered, or until sauce is reduced to about 4 cups. If you want to make sauce a day or so ahead, store, covered, in refrigerator.

A Pasta Party for Six to Eight People

Spaghetti is the heart of this meal, and with it you offer four distinctive sauces.

Antipasto: French bread and butter, plus an assortment of canned anchovies, marinated artichoke hearts, marinated mushrooms, or pickled Italian-style vegetables.

Assorted cold sliced meats such as dry salami, Genoa-style salami, mortadella, prosciutto, zampino, galantina, coppa.

Teleme or jack cheese in a chunk to cut.

Spaghetti: with Carbonara Sauce (page 33), Meatballs in Marinara Sauce (page 32), Garlic Sauce (page 32), and Pesto Sauce (1 cup of the sauce on page 29 or 2 packages—4 oz. size—frozen pesto) or Artichoke Sauce (page 34).

Raw vegetable salad basket: cut and eat portions.

Dessert: Fresh fruit, Italian cookies, and confections with espresso coffee.

To begin, offer the antipasto tray as a self-service course of cold meats and cheeses; allow 1 to 1½ pounds meats and at least 1 pound of cheese.

Then move guests in to the table, where the host introduces the pasta sampling by blending with showy dexterity spaghetti with the delicate Carbonara Sauce. After this round, guests are served or serve themselves to additional plain spaghetti (cook a total of 2 to 2½ lbs., drain, blend with 6 tablespoons melted butter and keep hot, covered, through the meal on an electric warming tray) and a selection of sauces. Each sauce is good separately or in combination with any of the others.

Have on the table a generous container of grated or shredded Parmesan for passing; it goes onto all the versions of spaghetti.

Jug wine is ideal throughout this meal; consider a red such as Barberone, Chianti, Burgundy, Claret, Zinfandel, or Vino Rosso.

Salad is a basket of fresh, crisp whole vegetables; have a knife handy for cutting off portions. Select vegetables such as peeled carrots, cauliflower, fennel (leave on feathery green tops), green onions with tops, green peppers, radishes, and zucchini.

Dessert might be a tray of fruit to eat out of hand such as tangerines, tangelos, peaches, apricots; include some Italian confections such as paneforte, torrone, and chocolates; and almond macaroons or other Italian cookies to go with espresso coffee.

Lasagne Belmonte

Thick tomato meat sauce and three kinds of cheese interspersed among the layers of wide lasagne noodles makes a delicious interpretation of the generally accepted notion as to what lasagne should be.

If you are so inclined, consider preparing fresh egg noodles (page 26) in wide lasagne ribbons for a superlative variation of this dish.

  1 **medium-sized onion, chopped**
  3 **tablespoons olive oil or salad oil**
1½ **pounds lean ground beef**
  1 **clove garlic, minced or mashed**
  2 **cans (8 oz. each) tomato sauce**
  1 **can (6 oz.) tomato paste**
 ½ **cup each dry red wine and water (or 1 cup water)**
    Salt
  1 **teaspoon oregano leaves**
 ½ **teaspoon each pepper and sugar**
12 **ounces lasagne noodles**
    Water
  1 **pound (2 cups) ricotta cheese or small curd cottage cheese**
 ½ **pound mozzarella cheese, thinly sliced**
 ½ **cup shredded Parmesan cheese**

In a large frying pan, sauté onion in oil until soft; add beef and garlic, and cook, stirring, until meat is brown and crumbly. Stir in tomato sauce, tomato paste, wine, and the ½ cup water. Add 1 teaspoon salt, oregano, pepper, and sugar, stirring until mixed. Cover pan and simmer slowly about 1½ hours.

Meanwhile cook noodles in boiling salted water as directed on the package, until tender, about 15 minutes. Drain thoroughly, rinse with cold water, and drain again. Arrange about ⅓ of the noodles in the bottom of a 9 by 13-inch shallow casserole dish, criss-crossing noodles to make an almost solid layer. Spread ⅓ of the tomato sauce over the noodles; top with ⅓ of the ricotta and mozzarella cheese. Repeat this layering two more times. Top with the Parmesan.

Bake, uncovered, in a 350° oven for 30 minutes. Remove from oven and cut in rectangles to serve. Makes 6 to 8 main dish servings.

Lasagne al Forno

Instead of layering the wide flat noodles with cheeses and sauce, here you make a rich cheese sauce, mix it with the noodles, then spoon meat sauce onto each portion. The casserole can be assembled ahead; bake it and reheat the meat sauce.

1 large onion, finely chopped
4 tablespoons each butter or margarine and all-purpose flour
1 can (14 oz.) regular strength beef broth
1½ cups milk
4 cups shredded fontina or tybo cheese
⅛ teaspoon ground nutmeg
10 ounces lasagne noodles, hot, cooked, and drained according to package directions
  Meat sauce (recipe follows), heated
1 cup or more freshly grated Parmesan cheese

Cook onion in butter, stirring, until soft but not browned. Blend in flour, remove from heat, and gradually stir in broth and milk. Return to high heat and cook, stirring, until boiling. Stir in 2 cups of the fontina cheese and nutmeg and remove from heat (you can cover and chill sauce, then reheat when ready to use).

Mix cheese sauce with well drained hot lasagne noodles and spread in a 3-quart shallow baking pan. With a fork lightly mix in 1½ cups of the warmed meat sauce. Cover noodles with remaining 2 cups fontina and 1 cup of the shredded Parmesan. (At this point you can cover and chill the casserole.)

Bake, uncovered, in a 375° oven for 20 minutes (30 minutes if chilled) until heated through. Spoon portions of lasagne onto individual plates and top generously with the remainder of the reheated meat sauce. Pass additional grated Parmesan if you like. Makes 6 to 8 main dish servings.

Meat sauce: Remove casings from about ¾ pound mild Italian pork sausages and crumble or coarsely chop meat. Combine meat with 1½ pounds lean ground beef in a wide frying pan or Dutch oven and add 1 large, finely chopped onion, 2 stalks diced celery, and 2 finely chopped carrots.

Cook, stirring, over high heat until meat is slightly browned and juices are evaporated. Stir in 1 can (6 oz.) tomato paste, 1 can (14 oz.) regular strength beef broth, 1½ teaspoons basil leaves, and ½ teaspoon rosemary leaves.

Boil rapidly, stirring as needed, until liquid is evaporated. Use hot; or chill, covered, and reheat before serving.

Polenta

Polenta is a staple dish in certain areas of northern Italy, particularly around Venice and Florence. This coarsely ground corn meal is considered properly made mush when boiled in a brass pot (that tapers from a flaring rim to a narrow base) and stirred with a wooden spoon or stick until the polenta is so thick

it pulls from the side of the pan and the stick can stand upright without aid. It is served freshly made or the cold slices are grilled; both may be topped with butter and cheese, or a sauce.

6 cups water
  About 1 teaspoon salt
2 cups polenta
  About 3 tablespoons butter (optional)
  Grated or shredded cheese such as Parmesan, Romano, fontina, jack
  Sauce (optional); suggestions follow

Bring water and 1 teaspoon salt to boiling and gradually stir in the polenta. Gently simmer, stirring frequently to prevent sticking, for about 30 minutes or until mixture is very thick; use a long handled spoon as the mixture pops and bubbles and can burn you. Stir in 3 tablespoons butter, if you like, and add salt to taste, if needed.

Spoon from pan into a buttered bowl and let set for 10 minutes. Invert onto a flat plate; the mixture will unmold and hold the shape of the bowl. Traditionally you cut slices with a string held tautly. Cut polenta into thick slices and serve hot, topped with more butter, cheese, or any sauce in this chapter that is intended to spoon onto pastas.

To grill, cut cold polenta in slices about ¾ inch thick. Brush lightly on all sides with olive oil or melted butter and place on a grill about 4 or 5 inches over an even bed of medium hot coals. Cook 6 to 7 minutes on each side, or until lightly toasted and hot throughout. Makes 8 to 10 servings.

Basic Risotto

Risotto is rice cooked to develop a creamy, flowing consistency. Even in its plainest form, seasoned only with a little onion, garlic, broth, and cheese, risotto is distinctive and worthy of presentation as a first course dish, or as a course to follow antipasto. It is also an elegant companion for plainly roasted or grilled meats.

Particularly in northern Italy, there are many elaborations of the basic risotto, including such savory elements as mushrooms, truffles, saffron, shellfish, chicken livers, and chicken. In many cases the dish becomes substantial enough to make an entrée.

Parmesan is typically the cheese used in risotto, but Asiago and Romano make interesting substitutions. The flavor of the imported Romano is much sharper than the domestically made cheese, therefore we suggest using half as much of the imported cheese in the following risotto; then you can add more to taste as the risotto is served.

2 tablespoons each butter or margarine and
    olive oil
1 small or medium-sized onion, chopped
1 small clove garlic, minced or mashed
1 cup long grain rice or short grain California
    pearl rice
  About 3½ cups hot regular strength
    chicken or beef broth
  Salt to taste
½ cup freshly shredded or grated Parmesan,
    Asiago, or domestic Romano cheese (or ¼
    cup imported Romano)
  About 1 tablespoon butter or margarine
  Additional freshly grated or shredded
    Parmesan, Asiago, or Romano cheese

Heat the 2 tablespoons butter and olive oil together in a heavy saucepan (about 2-qt. size) or 10-inch frying pan with a tight-fitting lid. Add the chopped onion and sauté over medium heat until soft and golden, stirring. Add garlic and rice and stir until the rice is milky and opaque in appearance, about 3 minutes.

Next add 1 cup of the broth, reduce heat, cover, and simmer until most of the liquid has been absorbed, about 10 minutes. Add the remaining hot broth in 2 or 3 additions, removing cover each time and stirring lightly with a fork; cook until the rice is tender and most of the liquid has been absorbed, about 20 to 25 minutes longer. (Exact amount of liquid needed and cooking time varies with rice and cooking pan you use; also, short grain rice cooks a little faster.) Taste, and add salt if needed.

Remove from heat and add half the cheese and remaining 1 tablespoon butter; mix lightly with 2 forks. Turn into a serving dish or serve from the casserole, topping with remaining cheese. You may also pass extra cheese at the table. Makes 4 to 6 servings as a first course or accompaniment to meats.

Risotto with White Truffles:

Prepare the Basic Risotto, omitting the garlic and cooking the onion in 3 tablespoons butter. Use short grain California pearl rice and 3 cups chicken broth, adding to it the juice drained from 1 can (1 oz.) white truffles. When rice is almost tender, stir in ½ cup whipping cream. Slice the truffles paper thin. To finish, stir in the 1 tablespoon butter, ¾ cup grated Parmesan cheese, and about half the truffles. Pour into a serving dish and top with the balance of the truffles and sprinkle with about ¼ cup more of cheese.

Risotto alla Milanese:

Soak 5 large slices dried Italian mushrooms in hot water about 1 hour; rinse, drain, chop, and add to sauté with onions in the Basic Risotto recipe. (Or use about 4 medium-sized fresh mushrooms, chopped.)

Use chicken broth for the liquid. About 5 to 10 minutes before the rice is done, stir in with a fork ¼ teaspoon saffron, dissolved in ¼ cup Madeira, white wine, or chicken broth.

Risotto Verde:

Use the Basic Risotto recipe, except substitute 3 sliced green onions (including part of the tops) for the onion. While the rice is simmering, prepare this mixture: place 2 tablespoons butter or margarine in a frying pan over medium heat. Add 1 carrot, shredded, and 1 stalk celery, thinly sliced; cover and cook about 5 minutes. Add 2 cups finely chopped fresh spinach or Swiss chard and 2 tablespoons minced parsley; continue to cook, stirring several times, about 3 minutes; sprinkle with a dash of nutmeg and add vegetables to rice when it is about three-quarters done. Finish as for Basic Risotto, omitting the final 1 tablespoon butter.

Risotto alla Finanziera:

Prepare the Basic Risotto, using chicken broth. While it is simmering, prepare this sauce: heat 2 tablespoons butter or margarine in a frying pan. Add 1 medium-sized onion, chopped; sauté until onion is golden. Add 1 cup sliced fresh mushrooms, ½ pound chicken livers (cut in bite-sized pieces), ⅛ teaspoon *each* ground sage and crushed bay leaf, and ½ teaspoon salt; continue to sauté over medium heat about 5 minutes. Add ¼ cup dry Sherry or chicken broth; cook quickly until almost all liquid has been evaporated.

Stir half the sauce into risotto with the first addition of cheese, omitting the 1 tablespoon butter. Turn out onto a serving dish, making a well in the center of the risotto, add the remaining sauce to the well, then sprinkle with the remaining cheese. Makes about 4 main dish servings.

Meats

Veal, beef and pork, special dishes the Italian way

The Italian way with meats begins simply—they are served relatively unadorned from the grill, the spit, the oven, or the frying pan. From this point they go to delicately seasoned and sauced dishes or to those renowned for their robust character.

Some of the greatest subtleties are involved in the making and curing of sausages and hams. For example, prosciutto, the dry Italian ham, is regarded as just one kind of ham in this country. In Italy, though, a good delicatessen will offer at least a dozen prosciuttos, each distinctive from the other. Although these cured meats are delights in their own right, they are often used to season other foods.

VEAL

Thin scallops of veal, the base for several of the following recipes, all share the same preliminary preparation steps of trimming and pounding to a thin layer. Italians use tender young veal and can often achieve the same results merely by slicing the meat very thinly; our more mature veal benefits from the tenderizing effect of pounding. Pounding can be done as much as a day ahead, and the meat refrigerated until time for it to be quickly cooked.

How to trim and pound veal: You can use any piece of veal from the leg, loin, rib, or shoulder that is cut like a steak or chop (⅓ to ½ inch thick) or the thin boneless segments called scallops or scallopini; all will be of comparable tenderness. (Some of the following recipes specify steaks cut from the leg because you need the large shape.) If the price per pound of bone-in chops is half that of a boneless cut (or a small round bone leg steak), it is usually more economical to choose the chops.

Cut away any bone; reserve it for another use, such as soup stock. Following natural divisions, separate large steaks into smaller pieces. Closely trim away fat and all silvery colored connective tissue and membrane as it shrinks upon contact with heat and causes the meat to curl.

Place several pieces of veal at a time between two sheets of waxed paper, leaving room for the meat to expand to about three times its original surface area. Pound each piece gently but firmly by lifting a heavy, flat-surfaced mallet about 8 to 12 inches above the meat, then letting it fall squarely to flatten meat evenly to about 3/16-inch thickness (or thinner, if recipes specify). Replace waxed paper as it tears. Repeat until all meat is pounded. (A heavy wine bottle—held by the neck—or a rolling pin can substitute for the mallet but are cumbersome to use.)

Cook veal immediately or place slices side by side on waxed paper, stack in layers or roll, then wrap well. Refrigerate for up to one day.

Basic Veal Sauté

Veal cooked in this manner, with many variations in the finishing touches, is common throughout Italy. Appropriate complementary dishes would include vegetables such as hot cooked peas, zucchini, artichokes, new potatoes; or these vegetables served cold as a salad; or a green salad.

⅓ pound boneless veal for each serving,
    trimmed and pounded according to
    preceding directions
All-purpose flour
Butter, margarine, olive oil, or salad oil
Salt and pepper

Coat each piece of veal with flour, shake off excess, and lay pieces side by side until all are coated.

Allow 2 tablespoons fat for each pound of veal to be sautéed; butter and margarine add flavor and enhance browning but burn easily (a combination of butter and oil is flavorful and doesn't burn as readily).

Place a 10 to 12-inch frying pan over highest heat. When pan is hot, coat surface with about 2 teaspoons butter; as it begins to brown, add veal but do not crowd slices. Add butter, about 1 teaspoon at a time, as pan appears dry. As meat shrinks, move pieces close together and add more veal, keeping pan full at all times.

When edges of veal turn white, in about 1 minute, turn slices over and cook until lightly browned on the other side; takes about 1 more minute.

When veal is cooked, transfer to a platter and keep warm. Season with salt and pepper to taste and serve.

Scallopini Picatte:

Prepare 1⅓ pounds boneless veal according to Basic Veal Sauté, cooking the veal in butter. Squeeze the juice of 1 lemon over the cooked meat and garnish with lemon wedges. Makes 4 servings.

Veal Scallopini with Lemon:

Prepare 2 pounds boneless veal according to Basic Veal Sauté. When meat is cooked, add to the hot pan an additional 1 tablespoon butter or margarine, ¼ cup dry Vermouth, and 1 teaspoon grated lemon peel. Boil rapidly, stirring to free browned particles, until liquid is reduced about one third. Spoon sauce over meat and garnish with minced parsley and lemon slices. Makes 6 servings.

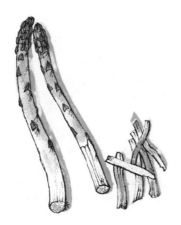

Veal Scallopini with Teleme:

Prepare 2 pounds boneless veal according to Basic Veal Sauté. After dusting the meat with flour, sprinkle with 1 teaspoon crushed oregano leaves, then sauté. As veal is cooked, arrange in overlapping slices on a heat-proof platter. Arrange thin slices of teleme cheese (about 5 oz. total) over meat; sprinkle with ¼ cup freshly grated Parmesan cheese. Broil 2 to 3 inches from heat just until cheese melts and is bubbly. Makes 6 servings.

White Scallopini

Fresh asparagus makes an elegant companion for this dish.

1½ pounds boneless veal, trimmed and
    pounded according to directions on
    page 43
½ cup all-purpose flour mixed with 1
    teaspoon salt and ⅛ teaspoon pepper
6 tablespoons butter or margarine
2 tablespoons salad oil
1 large onion, chopped
½ pound mushrooms, sliced
1 or 2 cloves garlic, minced or mashed
1 cup dry white wine
½ to 1 cup regular strength chicken broth
1 tablespoon lemon juice
½ teaspoon thyme leaves, crumbled
1 cup sour cream
2 teaspoons all-purpose flour

Dip pounded veal pieces in the seasoned flour to coat both sides; shake off excess flour. In a large frying pan, heat 3 tablespoons of the butter and the salad oil over medium high heat. Without crowding meat in pan, brown each piece quickly on both sides; set meat aside on a plate as it is browned.

Add remaining 3 tablespoons butter to pan and sauté the onion, mushrooms, and garlic over medium low heat for about 5 minutes. Stir in the wine, ½ cup chicken broth, lemon juice, and thyme. Return meat to pan, cover, and simmer gently for 15 minutes, to blend flavors. Blend the sour cream with the 2 teaspoons flour and stir into the meat mixture until blended. Return to simmering and serve. Or cool, then refrigerate; reheat slowly over low heat, stirring occasionally. Add a little more chicken broth if needed to thin the gravy slightly. Makes 4 to 5 servings.

Variation: For fewer calories, omit the sour cream and 1 tablespoon lemon juice; stir in 1 cup unflavored yogurt blended with the 2 teaspoons flour.

Veal Scallopini with Marsala

Swiss chard or spinach pair nicely with this veal sauté.

½ pound mushrooms
4 tablespoons (⅛ lb.) butter or margarine
1½ tablespoons lemon juice
1½ pounds boneless veal, trimmed and pounded according to directions on page 43
¼ cup all-purpose flour
1 teaspoon salt
¼ teaspoon pepper
¾ cup Marsala or dry Sherry
1 teaspoon beef stock base or 1 bouillon cube
1 tablespoon minced parsley

Slice mushrooms thinly. Melt 2 tablespoons of the butter in a large frying pan, add mushrooms, sprinkle with lemon juice, and cook on medium heat just until mushrooms are limp. Pour out of pan and set aside.

Cut veal into strips about 1 inch wide and dust in flour seasoned with salt and pepper; shake off excess. Melt remaining butter in the frying pan and brown meat on high heat, turning to brown both sides; set meat aside as browned. Pour in wine, add beef stock base, and cook rapidly, stirring constantly, until all browned particles are incorporated into sauce. Return mushrooms and meat to the pan and heat until hot through.

Serve at once, garnished with minced parsley. Makes 4 servings.

Veal Florentine

Spinach and cheese top sautéed veal; you can pound veal or buy prepared chopped veal steaks.

1 package (10 to 12 oz.) frozen chopped spinach
⅓ cup shredded Parmesan cheese
2 tablespoons fine dry bread crumbs
½ teaspoon spaghetti sauce seasoning mix (or mixed Italian herbs)
¼ teaspoon salt
1⅓ pounds boneless veal, trimmed and pounded as directed on page 43, or 4 chopped veal steaks (thaw, if frozen)
1 egg, slightly beaten
1 tablespoon each butter or margarine and salad oil
¼ pound Gruyère or Swiss cheese, shredded

Cook spinach according to package directions and keep warm. Meanwhile, mix together Parmesan cheese, crumbs, seasoning mix, and salt. Dip meat (remove butter patties from chopped veal, if present) in slightly beaten egg and then in the crumb mixture, coating all sides. Heat butter and oil in a large frying pan over medium heat, and brown meat on both sides; takes about 6 minutes. Transfer meat to an ovenproof platter.

Drain spinach well, pressing out excess moisture, then mix with Gruyère cheese and place an equal size mound on each piece of meat. Broil just until cheese melts. Makes 4 servings.

Saltimbocca Stuffed with Cheese

Don't be surprised to learn that the name of this sautéed veal and ham dish roughly translates as "jump in mouth." The name fancifully suggests—and rightfully so—that the dish is delectable.

Prosciutto and cheese are the flavors that distinguish this preparation of thin sheets of veal from scallopini. The most typical way of assembling saltimbocca is to roll the veal around the ham and cheese; but, as you might expect, there are variations.

4 veal round steaks, each cut ½ inch thick (about 2 lbs.)
24 very thin slices prosciutto (about 6 oz.)
¼ pound fontina (or Swiss) cheese, cut in 12 sticks
4 tablespoons butter or margarine
¼ teaspoon each sage leaves and basil leaves
½ teaspoon prepared English (hot) mustard or Dijon-style mustard
⅓ cup dry white wine
Hot, cooked, and buttered egg noodles (optional)

Trim and pound meat according to directions on page 43. Divide meat into 12 pieces of fairly equal size (join scraps into larger pieces by overlapping edges and pounding between sheets of waxed paper; handle gently). Top each piece of veal with several slices of prosciutto and a piece of cheese. Roll meat to enclose filling completely, turning in the sides; secure with small skewers.

Melt butter in a large frying pan over high heat, and blend in sage, basil, and mustard. Add meat rolls and brown quickly on all sides, turning frequently; takes 4 to 5 minutes. Remove rolls, add wine to pan, scraping browned particles free. Pour sauce over veal, and serve meat with noodles. Makes 6 servings.

Layered Saltimbocca:

This is essentially the same dish as the Saltimbocca Stuffed with Cheese, but the meat is not wrapped around the filling. Instead, it forms the base for layers of prosciutto and cheese. Use the preceding proportions. Trim and pound the meat as directed. Prepare the butter mixture; brown flat pieces of veal, allowing about ½ minute for each side.

Place meat, as cooked, on a rimmed baking sheet. Top each piece with sliced prosciutto and slices of the fontina cheese. Heat in a 375° oven for about 4 minutes, or until cheese melts. In the meantime, add wine to cooking pan and boil to reduce about half. Arrange saltimbocca on serving tray; combine juices from baking sheet with the reduced sauce and pour over meat, or pass at table to pour over each portion. Serve with hot cooked, buttered noodles, or steamed rice. Makes 6 servings.

Osso Buco

Braised veal shanks, with a succulent treasure of marrow in the bones, makes a superlative stew. New potatoes, peas, and sautéed tiny mushrooms complement this lemon and garlic flavored, Milanese style osso buco. A contrasting style of this dish made in the south of Italy is seasoned with tomatoes and sweet spices such as cinnamon.

    7 to 8 pounds meaty slices of veal shank
       with marrow in the bone, cut in
       2-inch-thick slices (12 to 18 pieces)
       Salt and all-purpose flour
    6 tablespoons butter or margarine
    1½ cups dry white wine
    ¾ to 1½ cups chicken broth (regular
       strength, canned, or freshly made, or
       Brown Stock, page 19)
    1½ tablespoons grated lemon peel
    ½ cup minced parsley
    1 medium-sized clove garlic, mashed

Sprinkle shanks with salt, then roll in flour, shaking off excess. Melt butter in a large heavy kettle and brown shanks on all sides; remove browned pieces from pan to prevent crowding. Return all meat to pan, add wine and ¾ cup of the broth, cover, and simmer gently for 2 to 2½ hours or until meat is very tender when pierced; add more broth if sauce becomes too thick. (You can cook meat the day before, cool, cover, and refrigerate overnight. Reheat slowly for 30 to 45 minutes before serving.)

Carefully remove meat to a warm platter (keep sections whole) and put in a warm place. Bring sauce to a rolling boil, scraping free browned particles; add a little more broth if needed. Mix lemon peel, parsley, and garlic. Add half this mixture to sauce and let simmer several minutes; garnish meat with remaining lemon peel mixture. Salt to taste. Pour sauce over the meat or serve separately to be ladled on as desired. Makes 6 to 8 servings.

Fritto Misto

In the south of Italy, or anywhere along the lengthy coastline, fritto misto is usually a combination of crisply fried fishes. But in the north and inland it is more likely to be this combination of veal, other meats, and vegetables, which, all together, make a whole meal.

Fritto Misto can be a remarkably light and delicate dish, and even though it is usually regarded as family fare, guests would enjoy such a treat. The engineering of this fritter meal is simpler than you might first think. You need only a small portion of each item, and all the preparation of meats and vegetables must be completed before you begin cooking. Keep the fritters warm in the oven, draining on absorbent material while the remaining foods cook, then serve them all at the same time. (The fritters can also be reheated.) The menu is completed by the addition of a green salad and crusty bread. An appropriate dessert might be spumone or a rum-flavored cake.

These proportions serve 8 to 10. Use smaller amounts of each ingredient to make fewer servings.

    1¼ to 1½ pounds boneless veal
    4 or 5 chicken thighs (not including
       drumsticks)
    1 set of beef brains (about ¾ lb.)
    1 pound veal sweetbreads (optional)
    4 or 5 whole chicken livers (about ¼ lb.)
    3 medium-sized zucchini
    3 small crookneck squash
    1 small regular (about 1 lb.) eggplant or 2
       Italian eggplant
    4 or 5 small artichokes (each 2½-inch
       diameter or less) or 10 to 12 thawed,
       frozen artichoke hearts
       Vinegar and water
    16 to 20 small mushrooms (caps should be
       about ½ inch in diameter)
       Salt
       All-purpose flour
       About 6 beaten eggs
       Olive oil or salad oil, or half butter and
       half oil
       About 4 or 5 lemons

Prepare each of the foods for cooking as follows: trim and pound veal according to directions on page 43.

Remove skin from chicken thighs and cut out the bone, if desired; cut each thigh lengthwise into 2 or 3 portions. Peel membrane from brains and sweetbreads with your fingers and rinse meats well in water, cut in slices about ½ inch thick. Cut each chicken liver in half.

Cut zucchini into diagonal slices, each about ⅜ inch thick. Cut the crookneck squash into lengthwise slices, each about ¼ inch thick. Slice eggplant crosswise into pieces about ¼ inch thick, or cut lengthwise into sticks that are about ⅜ inch thick. Break all tough outer leaves from artichokes, cut off the top ⅓ (removing all thorns), and trim stem end. Cut each artichoke in half or quarters and place immediately in acid water (1 tablespoon vinegar to each 1 quart of water). Drain well to use. If necessary, slice the discolored end from stems of the washed and drained mushrooms. Season all of these foods by sprinkling them with salt.

To cook, turn each piece in the flour and shake off excess, then dip into the beaten egg.

Fry over medium high heat in a wide frying pan containing about ½ inch of hot olive oil (or half oil, half butter) until each piece is richly browned. Add more fat as needed, spooning out the small browned particles as they accumulate. Fry the vegetables first, then the meats, and last of all the veal; cook veal just enough to brown lightly. Remove browned pieces from the pan and place on baking sheets lined with absorbent material; keep warm in about a 150° oven.

To save space you can top the first layer of fritters with more absorbent material, then drain additional fritters on this layer. When every piece is cooked, transfer the fritters to warmed platters or napkin-lined baskets; it's a good idea to keep each kind grouped for identification; without tasting this can be confusing. Squeeze the juice of at least ½ lemon (a juicy one) over each serving. These fritters, spread out in a single layer, can also be reheated in about 5 to 8 minutes in a 350° oven. Makes 8 to 10 servings.

Veal Indorato:

This veal dish is a less bountiful version of Fritto Misto. To make 6 servings, prepare and serve as directed for Fritto Misto, using 6 small artichokes, 2 or 3 medium-sized zucchini, 1 small eggplant, and 1½ pounds boneless veal.

Vegetable Fritters:

Choose any of the vegetables used for Fritto Misto and prepare in the quantity desired to serve as a side dish to go with plainly cooked meats.

Vitello Tonnato

This simmered chunk of veal, a classic summer dish when served with tuna sauce, is perfect for a buffet meal. Serve with a well seasoned rice salad and sliced tomatoes.

4 - pound piece veal leg, boned and butterflied
3 or 4 canned anchovy fillets
1 cup chopped onion
½ cup sliced carrot
½ cup sliced celery
2 cloves garlic
1 teaspoon salt
Herb bouquet of 2 teaspoons crushed bay leaf, 2 teaspoons thyme leaves, and 5 or 6 sprigs parsley tied in a square of cheese cloth
Water and dry white wine
Tuna sauce (recipe follows)

Lay out the boned meat as flat as possible and place the anchovies on the meat. Then, starting with a narrow end of the meat, roll it up tightly. Tie firmly with cotton string in 3 or 4 places. Set meat in a deep, close-fitting kettle. Add onion, carrot, celery, garlic, salt, herb bouquet, and enough water and wine, in equal quantities, to barely cover meat. Bring to a boil, cover, and simmer gently for 1 hour and 15 minutes or just until meat is easily pierced with a fork. Let meat cool in stock. Lift meat from pan and pour stock through a wire strainer, reserving it and discarding residue. Return meat to the kettle, and add all but ¼ cup of the stock (reserve for the tuna sauce) to the pan; chill meat at least 12 hours. Transfer meat to a serving platter (save the stock for soup or other uses). Slice thinly and accompany with tuna sauce. Makes 8 to 10 servings.

Tuna sauce: Whirl in a covered blender until smooth 2 cans (about 7 oz. *each*) tuna, 8 canned anchovy fillets, 3 tablespoons lemon juice. Gradually add 1 cup olive oil, blending at low speed until thick and smooth. Blend in the reserved ¼ cup cooking stock. Pour into a serving bowl and stir in 2 tablespoons capers; chill, covered, until ready to serve.

Spinach Stuffed Veal Breast

What breast of veal lacks in meatiness is made up for by this savory meat stuffing. Carrots contrast colorfully as a side dish.

If you like, skim the fat from the roasted meat juices, dilute with a little water, and bring to a boil, stirring to free browned particles. Then thicken as much as you like with a water-cornstarch paste and serve as a sauce with the meat.

- 1 tablespoon olive oil
- ¼ pound each ground veal and cooked ham (or all veal or all ham)
- 3 slices bacon, finely chopped
- 1 cup finely chopped onion
- 1 large garlic clove, minced
- 1 teaspoon basil leaves or tarragon leaves
- ⅓ cup finely chopped parsley
- ½ pound mushrooms, finely chopped
- 2 pounds fresh spinach, cooked, chopped, and well drained
- ¾ cup shredded Gruyère cheese
- 1 cup soft bread crumbs
- 1 egg
- 1½ teaspoons salt
- ¼ teaspoon pepper
- 3½ to 4-pound veal breast, split to form a pocket for stuffing
  Butter or salad oil
  Basil leaves or tarragon leaves, thyme leaves, and bay leaf

Heat olive oil in a large frying pan; add ground meats and bacon and cook until browned. Add onion, garlic, basil, and parsley to meat mixture and continue cooking until onions are soft, about 10 minutes, stirring constantly. Remove from heat and combine with mushrooms, spinach, cheese, bread crumbs, egg, salt, and pepper; mix until thoroughly combined. Pack stuffing lightly into veal breast; fasten meat securely with small skewers, or sew with string to hold stuffing inside. Place meat, fat-side up, in pan; rub with butter or salad oil and sprinkle lightly with crumbled basil, thyme, and bay leaf. Cover pan and bake for 2¼ hours in a 350° oven; remove cover and bake for about 15 minutes longer to brown surface. Remove skewers or string, and slice between bones to serve. Makes 6 to 8 servings.

BEEF AND PORK

The prize beef dish of Italy is the Florentine steak from the cattle of Tuscany. Usually it is a thick por-

terhouse (but always some tender cut), grilled rare over glowing coals. If seasoned at all, olive oil is brushed on while the meat cooks, or a pat of butter is added when served, plus a generous squeeze of lemon juice, and salt to taste.

Roasts are also greatly favored as the main fare of a meal, particularly when other parts of the menu are richly seasoned. An impressive offering in many restaurants is the hot roast cart, wheeled about to give diners a close up choice of roasts (bone-in or boneless rolls) of beef, pork, veal, kid, lamb, chicken, turkey, and frequently game. The meat may have cooked in an oven or all together on a huge spit, with only the natural juices plus a few herb leaves and olive oil to make them perfectly delicious.

Another popular (though plain) preparation of meats is the bollito misto, or mixture of boiled meats, such as whole beef brisket, tongue, and other less tender cuts of meat, poultry, and sausages that cook together. They may be served hot or cold, plain or with sauce.

Braised Chuck Roast

Spoon some of this rich sauce over hot boiled rigatoni or large shell macaroni.

- 3 to 4-pound beef chuck roast
- 1 large onion, chopped
- 2 tablespoons olive oil
- 3 cans (8 oz. each) tomato sauce
- 1 can (6 oz.) tomato paste
- 1 cup water
- ½ teaspoon each ground allspice, poultry seasoning, and thyme leaves
- 6 cloves garlic, minced or mashed
- ¼ cup chopped parsley
- ½ pound mushrooms, sliced, or 1 can (6 oz.) whole mushrooms, drained
  Salt and pepper to taste

In a Dutch oven or large frying pan, slowly brown the meat and onions in oil. Then add tomato sauce, tomato paste, water, allspice, poultry seasoning, thyme, garlic, and parsley. Cover and simmer slowly for 1½ to 2 hours until meat is tender when pierced. About 15 minutes before serving, add the mushrooms and continue to simmer. Makes 6 to 8 servings.

Green Pea Stew

This stew begins with a homemade sauce and is easiest to eat if served in wide, rimmed bowls.

1½ pounds cubed beef stew meat
¾ teaspoon salt
2 or 3 tablespoons olive oil or salad oil
3 cups Meatless Italian Gravy (see page 30)
6 cups shelled fresh peas (about 6 lbs.
    in pod) or 3 packages (10 oz. each)
    frozen peas

Sprinkle meat with salt. In a wide heavy saucepan, brown meat in oil. Add gravy and peas. Cover and simmer gently for about 1 hour and 15 minutes or until meat is tender; stir occasionally. Makes 6 servings.

Eggplant with Mozzarella Cheese

Known by several names, this dish will also appear on a menu as melanzane con mozzarella or eggplant Parmigiano. It can be made well ahead of time, then baked to serve.

2 medium-sized eggplants (about 1 lb. each)
    All-purpose flour
2 eggs beaten with 4 tablespoons water
    Salad oil
    Meat sauce (recipe follows)
1 pound mozzarella cheese, sliced
½ cup grated Parmesan cheese

Cut eggplant into lengthwise slices about ¼ inch thick. Coat each slice with flour, shake off excess, and turn in egg mixture. Drain briefly and sauté in about ¼ inch salad oil over medium high heat until well browned and tender when pierced; use a large frying pan, adding oil as needed, and cook eggplant without crowding. When browned, drain thoroughly.

Line the bottom of a shallow 3 to 4-quart casserole with about half the eggplant. Spoon half the meat sauce over the top, covering it with about half the mozzarella cheese. Repeat with a layer of eggplant, then meat sauce, mozzarella cheese, and top with the Parmesan cheese. Cover and chill until time to bake.

Bake, uncovered, in a 375° oven until bubbly; takes about 40 minutes. Serve hot. Makes 8 to 10 servings.

Meat sauce: In a 4 or 5-quart saucepan, break apart 1½ pounds lean ground beef and add 1¼ to 1½ pounds thinly sliced mild Italian pork sausages, casings removed; 1 seeded green pepper, finely chopped; 2 medium-sized onions, chopped; and ½ pound mushrooms, chopped.

Cook over high heat, stirring frequently, until beef has lost its pink color. Add 1 can (about 1 lb.) whole tomatoes or pear-shaped Italian style tomatoes, 1 large can (15 oz.) tomato sauce, and 1 can (6 oz.) tomato paste. Simmer rapidly, uncovered, until sauce is very thick; about 45 minutes. Stir frequently. Remove from heat and let stand undisturbed until any fat rises to the surface, then skim it off and discard. Use sauce while hot or when cold; cover and chill for up to 4 days, or freeze.

Eggplant Lasagne:

Follow the directions for Eggplant with Mozzarella Cheese, making these changes: reduce mozzarella to ½ pound. For the meat sauce, brown 1½ pounds lean ground beef in its own fat with 2 chopped medium-sized onions. Stir in 1 teaspoon salt, ½ teaspoon oregano leaves, and 1 can (8 oz.) tomato sauce. Simmer, uncovered, for 10 minutes. Add 1 package (10 or 12 oz.) frozen chopped spinach and continue cooking until thawed. If necessary, skim fat from sauce. Layer the eggplant and meat sauce in a shallow 3-quart casserole; top with the mozzarella cheese. Cover and chill. Bake as directed. Makes 6 servings.

Castiglioni Stew

Full of vegetable chunks, this northern Italian stew starts with a prepared homemade sauce. Serve into wide, rimmed bowls.

1½ pounds cubed beef stew meat
3 tablespoons olive oil or salad oil
2 cups Meatless Italian Gravy (see page 30)
1 can (8 oz.) tomato sauce
1 can (about 14 oz.) regular strength
    chicken broth
3 medium-sized potatoes, cubed
4 carrots, cut in chunks
2 or 3 stalks celery, cut in chunks
1 can (about 7 oz.) pitted ripe or green ripe
    olives, drained
1 can (4 oz.) mushrooms and liquid
    (optional)
    About 1 teaspoon salt

In a large heavy saucepan brown meat in oil without crowding. Remove meat from pan and add gravy, tomato sauce, and broth. Let simmer for 10 minutes. Return meat to sauce along with potatoes, carrots, celery, olives, mushrooms, and mushroom liquid. Add salt to taste. Cover and cook slowly for about 2 hours, stirring occasionally. Makes 6 servings.

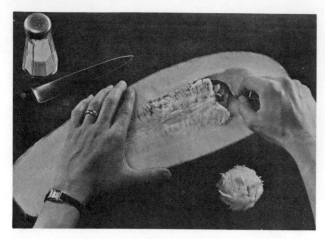

Scoop out fibrous material from large zucchini to make hollow to hold stuffing. Score flesh of the squash then add filling.

Zucchini Grande

It's a gardener's recipe, this zucchini dish. If you have a prolific zucchini vine in your garden, it is almost inevitable that in the late summer or fall you will discover a few squash of astonishing size. Stuffed and baked in the Italian manner, they can make a spectacular attraction at mealtime.

First test the zucchini for tenderness: if skins pierce easily with the tip of a sharp knife or your fingernail, they are good to eat. (As zucchini mature, they become hard outside, woody and fibrous inside, and are no longer edible.)

  Half a 5 to 8-pound zucchini (cut
    lengthwise)
4 tablespoons olive oil or salad oil
  Salt
1 large onion, finely chopped
1 pound lean ground beef
½ cup canned tomato sauce
½ teaspoon thyme leaves
¾ teaspoon salt
3 cups diced French bread cubes
  Water
1 package (12 oz.) frozen Swiss chard
½ cup lightly packed parsley
¼ cup shredded Parmesan cheese
3 eggs
  Additional shredded Parmesan cheese

Scoop soft, seedy center from zucchini half; discard. Score flesh in 1-inch squares, cutting half through to outer skin. Rub flesh with 2 tablespoons of the oil, sprinkle lightly with salt; set aside.

To make filling, heat remaining 2 tablespoons oil in a wide frying pan; add onion and cook until soft,

stirring. Add the meat, break apart with a spoon, and cook over high heat until no longer pink. Add tomato sauce, thyme, and ¾ teaspoon salt; simmer rapidly for about 5 minutes, stirring, then remove from heat.

Meanwhile cover the bread with water, then drain. With your hands, squeeze all water possible from bread, then set bread aside.

Combine chard and parsley with ½ cup water; bring to a boil, breaking up chard. Drain and cool. Squeeze out as much water as you can; chop greens fine.

Combine meat sauce, squeezed bread, chard, Parmesan cheese, and eggs, and beat to blend. Mound all the mixture into the zucchini, patting firmly in place.

Place zucchini in a baking pan with about ½ inch water. Bake, uncovered, in a 325° oven for about 1 hour 15 minutes or until quite tender all through. Supporting with two wide spatulas, transfer to a serving tray. Cut zucchini crosswise into serving portions. Pass the extra Parmesan cheese as topping. Makes 6 servings.

Pork and Olive Stew

This is another tasty stew that uses a homemade sauce as a starting point. It goes well with hot or cold broccoli spears.

2 pounds boneless lean pork cut in ¾-inch
    cubes (such as pork butt or shoulder)
2 to 3 tablespoons olive oil or salad oil
1-inch sprig fresh rosemary, or ¼ teaspoon
    rosemary leaves (optional)
1 clove garlic
2 cups Meatless Italian Gravy (see page 30)
¼ cup water
1 can (about 7 oz.) pitted ripe or green ripe
    olives, drained
¾ teaspoon salt

In a heavy frying pan, brown pork in oil; include a little pork fat, if there is any. Add rosemary, garlic, gravy, water, olives, and salt. Cover and simmer slowly about 1 hour, or until meat is tender; stir occasionally. Makes 6 servings.

Bollito Misto

Because it has green sauce (salsa verde) for its final embellishment, this bollito misto is Piedmontese-style.

Although generously scaled, bollito misto is easy to prepare; foods are added in sequence to one large kettle. Typically, the broth is served as a first course soup.

1 to 2 pounds veal or beef shank bones
1 stewing chicken (about 5 lbs.)
1 lean boneless beef roast (chuck, rump, or sirloin tip), about 3 pounds
1 coteghino sausage (1 to 1½ lbs.)
1 large onion, quartered
1 clove garlic
1 bay leaf
  About 3 quarts water
2 teaspoons salt
10 to 14 small new potatoes, peeled
12 to 16 small boiling onions, a cross cut in each root end
1 large head cabbage, cut in eighths
  Chopped parsley
  Salsa verde (recipe follows)

Arrange the bones in the bottom of a large pan (at least 8-qt. size). Place the chicken, beef roast, and sausage on top of the bones. Add large onion, garlic, and bay leaf; then add water until meats are three-quarters covered. Cover pan and bring to simmering. Simmer gently—or put into a 325° oven so the liquid continues to simmer very slowly—until meats are fork tender, about 3 to 4 hours.

After meats have cooked 1 hour, add the salt. About 1 hour before the meats are done, add the potatoes; 30 minutes later add the small onions. (You can tie each kind of vegetable loosely in a piece of cheesecloth when you add it to the pot; then you can lift the bag out when the vegetables are just tender to pierce and put them into a bowl with some of the broth and keep warm. Any of the meats that might get done before the others can also be lifted out and kept moist in a little broth. Just before serving, return everything to the pot to re-heat.)

Lift meats out of broth and arrange at one end of a large, deep platter. Arrange the vegetables at the other end of the platter. Cover and keep warm. Return broth to boiling, add the cabbage, and boil 6 to 8 minutes, uncovered, or until cabbage is just tender to pierce. Lift from broth with a slotted spoon and add to serving platter.

To serve the broth as a first course soup, pour it through a wire strainer and discard the residue. Skim off fat and discard. Pour broth into a tureen or individual bowls. Garnish the meat and vegetable platter with parsley. Carve the meats and serve some of each meat and each vegetable as a portion; pass salsa verde to spoon onto meats. Makes 10 to 14 servings.

Salsa verde: Combine the following ingredients in a blender jar and whirl, covered, until well blended:

½ cup olive oil; ¼ cup white wine vinegar; ½ small onion, cut up; 1 cup parsley; 2 tablespoons capers; 1 small clove garlic; 3 canned anchovy fillets; ½ teaspoon *each* oregano leaves, basil leaves, salt; and a dash pepper. Serve at room temperature.

Biroldo and Bean Sauté

Among the many European-style blood sausages, the sweetly spiced Italian type is distinguished by the addition of pine nuts and raisins. Although good cold, it is particularly tasty when warm and served with slowly cooked onions.

3 medium-sized onions, thinly sliced
½ teaspoon basil leaves
6 tablespoons butter
1 (1½ to 1¾ lbs.) biroldo ring sausage (or a length of the sausage)
2 packages (9 oz. each) thawed, frozen Italian green beans
2 tablespoons water
  Salt

Cook onions with basil in butter in wide frying pan over medium heat, stirring frequently, until onions are golden and with faint signs of browning.

Push onions to sides of the pan and lay the ring sausage in the center of the pan. Cover and cook gently for 10 to 12 minutes to heat sausage through; turn it over after the first 5 or 6 minutes. (An alternate method you can use if you prefer the sausage slightly crisp is to cut the uncooked sausage in 2-inch lengths, placing slices, cut sides down, in the pan with onions; cook, uncovered, for 10 to 12 minutes, turning once.) Transfer biroldo to a serving dish and keep warm. To pan add the beans and water. Cook over high heat, uncovered and stirring, until beans are hot and lightly cooked; takes about 3 minutes. Salt to taste and spoon beans with onions in and around sausage. Makes 6 servings.

Barbecued Italian Sausages

These sausages make delicious sandwiches on slices of Italian or French bread. Use regular mild or hotly seasoned Italian pork sausage links or the long Italian salsiccia vin blanc. If you use the salsiccia vin blanc, twirl in coils about 3 or 4 inches in diameter and secure with a wooden skewer through the diameter of the sausage, or cut the sausage in easily handled lengths.

Grill sausages about 6 inches above a bed of evenly ignited coals, turning as needed to brown well; grill for 30 to 40 minutes or until sausages are cooked to the center; cut a gash to test. Serve hot. Allow ⅓ pound for each serving.

Bollito Misto con Coteghino di Rapallo

Rapallo, where this dish originated, is a small town on the Mediterranean coast just south of Genoa. You may have to order the coteghino, a large fresh sausage, from an Italian delicatessen; it flavors the brisket, vegetables, and sauce.

Leftover meats are good reheated in a little butter.

> **About 5-pound piece fresh beef brisket**
> 2 **to 3 quarts water or meat broth (regular strength, canned, or freshly made)**
> 1 **each carrot, medium-sized onion, and celery stalk**
> 3 **or 4 parsley sprigs**
> 1 **bay leaf**
> 8 **to 10 whole black peppers**
> 4 **to 6 whole allspice**
>   **Salt**
> 1 **coteghino sausage (1 to 1½ lbs.)**
> 3 **to 4 large carrots, each cut in half**
> 6 **to 8 small whole potatoes, scrubbed**
> 6 **to 8 small, whole, boiling-size onions**
> 3 **to 4 large stalks celery, each cut in half**
>   **Chive sauce (recipe follows)**

Put the brisket in a large baking pan and bake in a 500° oven for 35 minutes; turn meat over after the first 25 minutes (add 3 or 4 tablespoons water to pan if drippings begin to char). Transfer brisket to a large deep kettle and rinse roasting pan with some of the water or broth to free all the browned particles. Add this liquid to meat plus enough more to total 2 to 3 quarts.

Add to pan the single carrot, onion, and celery stalk, parsley, bay leaf, peppers, allspice, and 2 tea-spoons salt (if cooking liquid is not salted). Bring to a boil, immediately reduce heat to a gentle simmer, and cover pan. Cook for about 2 hours; meat should feel slightly tender when pierced. Add the coteghino sausage and continue to simmer for 2 more hours.

Remove brisket and sausage from broth and keep in a warm place (such as a 150° oven) while you make sauce and cook remaining vegetables. Pour broth through a wire strainer; reserve broth and discard residue. Measure out and set aside 2 cups of the broth for the chive sauce.

Bring remaining broth to boiling. Add carrot halves, potatoes, and boiling onions; cook, uncovered, for 15 minutes. Add the celery; cook for another 5 minutes. Remove vegetables from broth with a slotted spoon. (Refrigerate this broth for soups or other uses.) Arrange brisket and coteghino on warm platter with vegetables. Slice meat to serve. Serve the chive sauce separately to pour over meat. Makes 8 generous servings.

Chive sauce: Cook 1 tablespoon minced shallots or green onions in 1 tablespoon butter or margarine over medium heat until soft but not browned. Blend in 2 tablespoons all-purpose flour; gradually add the reserved 2 cups strained cooking liquid. Simmer gently for about 10 minutes, stirring occasionally. Blend in 4 to 6 tablespoons minced chives (fresh, frozen, or freeze-dried) and 2 to 4 tablespoons half-and-half, or to taste for desired richness. Makes about 2 cups.

Salsiccia Vin Blanc with Risotto

You will probably have to visit an Italian delicatessen to get the long, continuously formed Italian white wine and pork sausage. It's usually somewhat more delicately seasoned than the regular mild Italian pork sausage, but the sausages can be used interchangeably in this recipe.

> 1½ **pound length of salsiccia vin blanc**
>   **Water**
> 2 **tablespoons butter**
> 1 **medium-sized onion, chopped**
> 1½ **cups California pearl (short grain) rice**
> 3½ **cups regular strength chicken broth**
> ½ **cup shredded Parmesan cheese**

Neatly coil the sausage in an 8 or 9-inch frying pan and add enough water to fill pan about ¼ inch. Prick sausage lightly in several places with a fork. Cover and simmer gently for 30 minutes. Drain off juices, cover, and brown sausage in its own fat over moderate heat, turning once; use a wide spatula to guide meat.

In the meantime, in another pan melt the butter and add onion and rice; cook over moderately high heat, stirring, until rice looks translucent and onion is slightly browned. Add broth and cook, loosely covered, over low heat for about 15 minutes, or until rice is tender to bite. Stir in the cheese and pour mixture into a serving dish; lay sausage on top and serve. Makes 6 servings.

Italian Sweet Sausage

If you can not buy mild Italian pork sausages, make these to use instead. In recipes that direct you to remove the casing, you can use the sausage mixture before it is shaped into lengths.

You will find the salted pig sausage casings in a meat market; ask your meat man for a single piece large enough for about 2 pounds of sausage. Soak the casings in warm water for 3 to 4 hours, then rinse in running water (slip one end over the faucet and let water run through casing); drain.

1 pound lean pork, cut in small pieces
½ pound fat pork, cut in small pieces
¾ teaspoon salt
1 teaspoon fennel seed
1 small clove garlic
¼ teaspoon freshly ground black pepper
½ teaspoon chile powder
   Salted pork sausage casings (freshen as directed above)

Grind lean pork and fat pork, forcing through the fine blade of a food chopper. Crush salt, fennel seed, garlic, pepper, and chile powder together in a mortar and pestle (or whirl seasonings in a covered blender jar). Blend seasonings with meat. Force meat through a sausage press into casing, or put meat in a large pastry bag (without a tip) and force into casing, making a plump sausage. Tie with string in 4 inch lengths. Hang in the air to dry for 3 to 4 hours; put in a place with a breeze (such as in front of a fan, but away from insects). Then refrigerate; use within 3 or 4 days. Makes about 1½ pounds.

VARIETY MEATS

Simple or bold seasonings, humble or elaborate presentations, and great appreciation characterize the Italian approach to the cooking of variety meats.

Beef Tongue, Tuscan-Style

The Italian name of this dish—Lingua Dolce-Forte—is an accurate description of it: tongue sweet-strong. In and around Florence, the art of balancing sweet with sharp in seasoning is popular. Here is an excellent example of the harmonious effect the contrasts can achieve together.

3¼ to 3¾-pound fresh beef tongue
6 cups water
3 large onions
4 carrots
6 to 8 parsley sprigs
½ cup olive oil
2 stalks celery, finely chopped
1 cup chopped parsley
2 tablespoons canned tomato paste
2 tablespoons minced candied citron or candied orange peel
½ cup raisins
2 tablespoons each sugar and all-purpose flour
½ ounce unsweetened chocolate, finely chopped
6 tablespoons wine vinegar
   Salt
⅓ cup pine nuts (pignoli)

Rinse tongue and place in a kettle with the water, 1 onion (quartered), 2 carrots (cut in chunks), and the parsley sprigs. Bring to a boil, cover, and simmer for 2½ to 3 hours or until tongue is easily pierced with a fork. Remove from heat and let stand in broth until cool enough to touch. Pour broth through a wire strainer and reserve. Discard vegetables.

Peel skin from tongue; trim off fat; remove any bones. Cut tongue crosswise in ¼-inch-thick slices; set aside.

Finely chop the remaining 2 onions and the 2 carrots. Combine in a wide frying pan with olive oil, celery, and chopped parsley, and cook, stirring, over medium heat for about 15 minutes or until vegetables are soft; do not brown.

Blend in tomato paste, citron, raisins, sugar, flour, and chocolate. Then mix in vinegar and 1 cup of the reserved broth (save balance for other uses). Bring to boil, stirring; remove from heat.

Sprinkle tongue lightly with salt, and season sauce to taste with salt; then layer meat and sauce into a 2-quart shallow casserole, finishing with a layer of sauce. Sprinkle with nuts. (At this point you can chill covered casserole.) Cover and bake in a 325° oven for 45 minutes (or 1 hour if chilled). Makes 6 to 8 servings.

Liver with Sauce

You find liver, seasoned in this manner, served in Naples. It does not require last minute frying.

¼ cup fine dry bread crumbs
2 tablespoons grated Parmesan cheese
¼ teaspoon garlic salt
⅛ teaspoon oregano leaves, crumbled
1 pound sliced beef liver, trimmed of tough membrane
Salt and pepper
1 egg, beaten
2 tablespoons each butter or margarine and olive oil or salad oil
4 ounces mozzarella cheese, sliced
1 can (8 oz.) tomato sauce
Finely chopped parsley

Combine in a shallow pan the bread crumbs, Parmesan, garlic salt, and oregano. Sprinkle each slice of liver lightly with salt and pepper; dip in beaten egg and drain briefly, then dip in the crumb mixture to coat on both sides. Heat the butter and oil in a frying pan until it is quite hot.

Fry the liver pieces quickly until browned on both sides, about 2 to 3 minutes. Drain, then alternate liver with mozzarella in a shallow baking dish (about 9 inches square). Pour tomato sauce over the top of the liver and cheese. Bake, uncovered, in a 350° oven for about 15 minutes. Serve immediately. Makes about 4 servings.

Venetian Liver with Onions

Venice, a seaport city famed for its fish dishes, also takes great pride in this preparation of liver.

4 large onions
½ cup olive oil
½ teaspoon grated lemon peel
2 pounds calf or baby beef liver, cut in ½-inch thick slices and trimmed of any tough membrane
All-purpose flour
Salt and pepper

Quarter onions and separate in layers. Place onion in a wide frying pan with oil and cook, stirring, over medium high heat for about 10 minutes or until onions are soft and slightly golden. Stir in lemon peel, then lift onions from oil with a slotted spoon and place in a bowl (this can be done several hours ahead; hold at room temperature, covered).

Coat liver with flour and shake off excess; lay pieces side by side on waxed paper as floured, then sprinkle with salt and pepper.

Return frying pan with oil (in which onions cooked) to medium heat and fill with liver slices; do not crowd. Brown liver well on both sides and cook until just a hint of pink color remains in the center (cut a gash to test); it takes about 5 minutes. Transfer liver as cooked to a warm platter and keep warm (in a low oven or on an electric warming tray); return onions to pan when liver is cooked and stir to heat through. Pour onions over liver and serve. Makes 5 to 6 servings.

Trippa alla Fiorentina

A Florentine cook tells us that to cook in the Florentine style, you must learn to begin with some onion, carrot, and celery, chopped fine. This mixture is the beginning of the richly flavored tomato sauce that coats slivers of tripe.

1½ pounds plain or honeycomb tripe
3 quarts water
2 large onions, minced
2 cloves garlic, minced
1 stalk celery, minced
3 carrots, minced
6 tablespoons olive oil
1 cup minced, lightly packed parsley
1 large can (1 lb. 13 oz.) whole tomatoes
1 can (6 oz.) tomato paste
½ teaspoon rosemary leaves
1 can (14 oz.) regular strength beef broth
Salt

Rinse tripe and place in a kettle with water. Cover and bring to a boil; simmer for 2 hours or until tripe is very easy to pierce.

Meanwhile, cook onions, garlic, celery, and carrots with olive oil in a wide frying pan over medium heat, stirring frequently, until vegetables are soft but not browned. Blend in parsley, tomatoes and liquid (breaking apart with a spoon), tomato paste, rosemary, and beef broth. Boil, uncovered, stirring occasionally, until quite thick; then stir more frequently to prevent scorching until the sauce is reduced to 3½ cups. Set aside.

Drain cooked tripe; when cool enough to handle, cut in slivers ⅛ to ¼-inch wide. Mix tripe with sauce and add salt to taste (at this point mixture can be covered and refrigerated overnight). Spoon tripe into a shallow 2-quart casserole or baking pan. Bake, uncovered, in a 425° oven for 45 minutes (if chilled, allow 50 minutes total cooking time) or until top gets slightly crusty and browned. Serves 5 to 6.

Poultry

Chicken and turkey, rustic to elegant

Chicken dishes are as commonplace in Italy as they are here, but the quality that makes them Italian style, whether homey or elegant, lends freshness to any meal.

Although we generally regard turkey as a whole roast, Italians are more likely to divide it into parts. The breast is often the base of delicate entrées.

Chicken and Mushrooms

Lucca provides this succulent combination of flavors; it goes together quickly and is good reheated. A delicious side dish is artichoke hearts and zucchini cooked as fritters (see page 46).

> 2½ to 3-pound broiler-fryer chicken, cut in serving pieces
> Salt
> Pepper
> 4 tablespoons olive oil
> 1 pound small mushrooms (or large mushrooms, sliced)
> 1 small onion, minced
> ⅓ cup (part of an 8 oz. can) tomato sauce
> ¼ cup water
> ½ cup chopped parsley
> 6 to 8 ounces vermicelli, hot, cooked, and drained (optional)
> 1 tablespoon butter (optional)
> Additional chopped parsley

Sprinkle chicken with salt and pepper. Place oil in a wide frying pan over medium heat and brown chicken on all sides; do not crowd pan. Remove chicken as browned and set aside.

To pan drippings, add mushrooms and onion and cook, stirring, until onion is soft. Return chicken to pan and add tomato sauce, water, and the ½ cup parsley. Cover and simmer for 40 minutes or until chicken is very tender; if, after 20 minutes, the chicken is quite soupy, remove lid and let sauce reduce while chicken continues cooking.

Serve with the hot noodles mixed with butter. Garnish with chopped parsley. Makes 3 or 4 servings.

Chicken and Olive Sauté

Only the dark pieces of chicken are used in this dish. Swiss chard is served with it to soak up some of the good sauce.

> ¼ cup olive oil
> 1 medium-sized onion, chopped
> 2 whole garlic cloves
> 6 chicken drumsticks and thighs, separated
> Salt
> ½ cup (part of an 8 oz. can) tomato sauce
> ¼ cup water
> 1 can (7½ oz.) pitted green ripe or ripe olives, drained
> 1 jar (2¼ oz.) pimiento-stuffed Spanish style olives, drained
> 2 packages (12 oz. each) frozen Swiss chard

In a large frying pan over moderate heat, cook the onion and garlic, stirring, until onion is soft; remove from pan with a slotted spoon and set aside.

Sprinkle chicken with salt, then brown lightly on all sides in the frying pan over moderately high heat. Return the onion and garlic to pan, then add the water and both kinds of olives. Cover pan and simmer gently for 40 minutes or until chicken is quite tender when pierced.

Just before the chicken is done, cook the chard according to package directions and drain well.

In a large serving dish, spoon the chard onto each side, then spoon the chicken in the center and pour the hot sauce over all. Makes 6 servings.

Chicken Scallopini

Chicken breasts or thighs, boned and pounded, seem remarkably like veal prepared for sautéing or scallopini. Any preparation or sauce you like for sautéed veal (page 43) can be used with the chicken. For each serving allow about 1 pound chicken breast (2 small or 1 large whole breast) or 2 thighs. Bone and skin; if breasts are whole, cut in halves.

Place pieces of meat on a large sheet of waxed paper (do a few pieces at a time), arranging 5 or 6 inches apart. Cover with waxed paper and pound meat firmly with a flat-surfaced mallet until each piece is 2½ to 3 times larger in size. Occasionally you will need to replace paper as it tears. Take care to avoid breaking meat apart with uneven blows.

Gently ease chicken from paper. Cook at once or transfer to fresh waxed paper, laying out smoothly in a single layer; wrap and chill.

To season, sprinkle lightly with salt; you can also dust sparingly with a crumbled dried herb such as basil leaves, rubbed sage, dill weed, oregano leaves, or marjoram leaves; seasoned pepper; or seasoned salt (omitting plain salt).

To cook, melt only enough butter or margarine in a frying pan to coat bottom. Over high heat cook chicken, without crowding, just until edges turn light. Turn and cook until meat changes from pink to white throughout and begins to brown lightly; takes 1 to 1½ minutes. Add butter to pan when needed to prevent sticking (but in small quantities because butter burns if used too generously). Keep meat warm as cooked. Accompany with lemon wedges to squeeze over if desired.

Chicken San Marino

Chicken breasts, pounded thin, are wrapped around ham and cheese, and coated with a crumb mixture; this can be done ahead. When the chicken is browned and served hot, the melted cheese flows from the center.

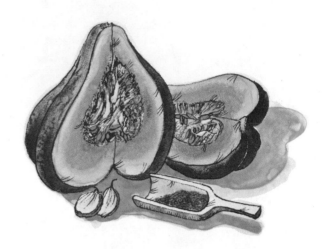

6 whole chicken breasts (about 1 lb. each), boned, skinned, and cut in half, then pounded as directed for Chicken Scallopini (see preceding recipe)

12 slices Gruyère or fontina cheese, each ¼ inch thick and in rectangles 1 by 2½ inches

12 very thin slices prosciutto or Westphalian ham

1 to 2 eggs, well beaten
  Salt and all-purpose flour
  Fine dry bread crumbs

4 to 6 tablespoons butter

3 tablespoons cognac

½ cup whipping cream

On each half of chicken breast, lay a portion of cheese wrapped in a slice of ham. Wrap the chicken around the ham, enclosing completely. Sprinkle rolls with salt, then coat with flour and shake off excess. Dip each roll in egg then roll in the bread crumbs. Set rolls side by side without touching (or refrigerate, covered, for several hours).

Melt 4 tablespoons butter in a wide frying pan large enough to hold the rolls. Cook on moderate heat, browning evenly and well on all sides, about 15 minutes; add more butter as needed to keep rolls moist. Transfer to a heat-proof serving dish, arranging rolls in a single layer. Bake in a 350° oven for 15 minutes, uncovered.

To the pan in which the chicken cooked, add the cognac and, at once, set aflame; shake pan to burn off the alcohol. Pour in the cream and boil until slightly thickened and large shiny bubbles form. Pour sauce over chicken and serve. Makes 6 servings.

Pollo Toscano

Make this fancy chicken casserole ahead of time.

3 - pound broiler-fryer chicken, cut in pieces
   (giblets optional)
1 whole chicken breast (about 1 lb.)
   Salt
2 tablespoons each olive oil and butter
   Stuffed mushrooms (recipe follows)
¼ cup chopped onion
1 large peeled, seeded, and diced tomato
½ teaspoon basil leaves
⅛ teaspoon rosemary leaves
½ cup each dry white wine and water
¼ cup minced prosciutto or cooked ham
8 ounces vermicelli or other thin noodle,
   hot, cooked, and drained
   Minced parsley

Bone the chicken breasts and thighs and cut meat in large pieces. Reserve bones, neck, and back of chicken for stock, if you wish; salt remaining pieces. Heat oil and butter in a large frying pan. Brown wings, drumsticks, thighs, gizzard, and heart on all sides, then push to a corner of the pan to continue cooking. Lightly brown pieces of breast and liver (they should remain pink inside), removing from pan as cooked; do not crowd. Remove all chicken from pan; set aside. In same pan brown bases of stuffed mushrooms; carefully set aside.

To the same drippings add onion, tomato, basil, and rosemary, and cook until onion is soft. Add wine and water and boil rapidly until reduced about half. Return chicken and any juices to pan, add prosciutto, and simmer 10 minutes.

Put chicken in a 2 to 3-quart casserole, top with mushrooms, and add sauce. Cover and chill at this point, if you wish.

Bake in a 375° oven for 30 minutes (40 minutes if chilled) or until chicken is tender when pierced. To serve, set mushrooms around edge of platter, swirl noodles in center, top with chicken, and pour sauce over all. Sprinkle with parsley. Makes 4 or 5 servings.

Stuffed mushrooms: Select 8 mushrooms, each about 2 inches in diameter; remove stems and scoop out centers. Mince stems and centers; cook in 1 tablespoon melted butter with ¼ cup minced onion until vegetables are soft. Cook ½ pound sweetbreads for 10 minutes in boiling salted water to cover. Drain; peel off membrane. Put sweetbreads through fine blade of a food chopper, then blend with cooked mixture, ⅓ cup shredded Parmesan cheese, ¼ cup chopped prosciutto or cooked ham, and salt to taste. Stuff all the filling into mushroom caps.

Chicken in a Pot

Birds cooked in a ceramic pot (see page 58) should fit the container closely, and the space between the meat and the pot should be no more than ½ inch. You can truss a big bird to fit a somewhat smaller pot, but remember that the pot's top must fit on tightly.

To ensure a good fit, take your cooker to market when you shop for the poultry.

2 to 3-pound broiler-fryer chicken
   Salt and pepper
1 medium-sized onion, quartered
1 clove garlic, minced or mashed
1 teaspoon salt
½ teaspoon rosemary leaves, crumbled
1½ tablespoons lemon juice

Sprinkle inside of the chicken cavity lightly with salt and pepper. Put onion inside body cavity and skewer cavities shut. Truss chicken with cord to fit compactly inside pot. Combine the garlic, 1 teaspoon salt, and rosemary; pat over bird. Pour the lemon juice over the top, cover, and bake in a 450° oven for about 45 minutes to 1 hour, or until tender. Makes 2 to 3 servings.

For a 4 to 6-pound roasting chicken: Follow the Chicken in a Pot recipe, but use 1 large onion, 1 large clove garlic, 1½ teaspoons salt, ¾ teaspoon rosemary leaves, and 3 tablespoons lemon juice. Truss to fit inside cooking pot. Bake in a 450° oven for about 1 hour and 15 minutes or until tender.

For a 5 to 7-pound turkey: Follow Chicken in a Pot recipe but double seasoning ingredients. Bake in a 400° oven for about 45 minutes to 1 hour. Insert a meat thermometer into thickest part of breast at end of cooking time; it should read about 175° after 3 minutes.

For a 10 to 13-pound turkey: Follow Chicken in a Pot recipe but omit seasoning other than salt and pepper. So that you may later remove the turkey easily, set a string harness (3 strands of cotton string, each 45 inches long, knotted together in the middle) so that the knot rests on the bottom of the pot and the ends extend over the edge. Set turkey in pot and tie the ends of the string together on top of the bird. Cover and bake in a 425° oven until the drumstick meat feels soft. Start testing in about 2½ hours; a meat thermometer in thickest part of the breast should register 175° when turkey is done.

Remove turkey from oven and reset oven temperature to 450°. Uncover pot and use a knife to gently

Lift off top of ceramic cooker at the table to reveal a golden brown chicken, roasted until tender and juicy.

Hot Pot Cookery

An old-fashioned Italian cooking utensil is the covered ceramic pot that looks like a snub nosed egg, and is irregularly split on the horizontal. However, there are many whimsical variations of pots in the form of ovals, fish, chickens, and the like. All the pots can be used as you would any casserole with a lid, but whole fowl can be cooked inside them producing interesting, showy results. Foods cooked this way are especially succulent and flavorful yet can be richly browned and tender. They require little attention in the oven, and can be kept moist and hot inside the pots if dinner is delayed.

The secret of good browning with these pots is to choose meats that conform roughly to the shape of the pot, then cook them at the correct oven temperature.

Cooking times are approximate as it will take longer to heat especially heavy or thick pots. Unglazed or partially glazed pots need to be seasoned before their first use. Follow manufacturer's directions; or run hottest tap water into a sink or large container to completely immerse pot. Let stand 8 hours or overnight. Drain and allow to dry at least 8 hours (if the pot is highly glazed this is not necessary).

Reserve the pot for specific foods—such as only for fish or only for poultry—as flavors linger; however, this can be pleasant if flavors are basically the same as those of foods cooked in the pot previously.

Ceramic pots are vulnerable to sudden temperature change. Do not pour cold liquid into a hot vessel, or put a refrigerated pot directly into a hot oven. When you remove cooking pots from the oven, set on a board or asbestos mat.

If your cooker cracks or breaks, you can probably repair it with a silicone glue by following directions on the package.

free any skin that is stuck to the pot. Transfer turkey with harness to another pan; remove trussing string. Pour out any juices; scrape free any particles that remain in pot, then blend these juices with turkey juices; reserve. Return turkey to pot and roast, uncovered, in the 450° oven until well browned, about 15 minutes. Siphon out any more juices and keep turkey warm in covered pot.

Combine all juices; skim off fat and reserve. Measure juices, adding, if needed, enough more regular strength chicken broth or water to make 3 cups.

Pour ½ cup of the reserved fat into a frying pan; add ½ cup all-purpose flour and cook, stirring, until flour is a toasty brown color (not scorched). Remove from heat and gradually stir in the turkey juices. Then bring to a boil, stirring, until thickened. Season with salt and pepper to taste.

Lift turkey onto a serving platter and cut away string harness; carve and serve with the turkey juice sauce. Makes 10 to 14 servings.

Chicken Laurel

Inspired by an elaborate Roman chicken dish served in a wreath of laurel leaves set aflame, this one is less complicated but still offers a superb blend of flavors. Bay is the predominant herb, but green peas, orange slices, and blazing, orange-flavored liqueur do much to dress up the crisply roasted chicken.

Fettucini would make a fine opening for this meal, and zabaglione would make a classic finish.

Use fresh bay leaves if you have access to *Umbelluria californica* (known as California laurel), California bay, pepperwood, or Oregon myrtle, depending upon where you live.

4½ to 5-pound roasting chicken
   Salt
½ large, unpeeled orange, cut in chunks
½ medium-sized onion, sliced
2 or 3 bay leaves
   About 2 tablespoons butter or margarine
¼ teaspoon grated orange peel
⅓ cup orange juice
2 or 3 cups hot cooked fresh peas or hot cooked frozen petite (or tiny) peas, drained
1 or 2 large oranges, peeled with white membrane removed, then sliced crosswise
   Small cluster fresh bay leaves (or 3 or 4 dried bay leaves)
3 tablespoons Cointreau or other orange-flavored liqueur

Remove giblets from chicken and set aside for other uses. Sprinkle chicken inside and out lightly with salt. Fill body and breast cavity with unpeeled orange chunks, the onion, and the 2 or 3 bay leaves.

Place chicken on a rack, breast side up, in a roasting pan and tuck the neck skin under the chicken. Skewer body opening shut, if you like.

Bake chicken in a 325° oven until leg moves easily when jiggled and skin is golden brown, about 2 to 2½ hours. After the first 30 minutes, rub chicken with a lump of butter to moisten the skin. Rub with butter once or twice more during the roasting period.

Protecting your hands with pot holders, tip cooked chicken to drain juices from the body into the roasting pan, then transfer chicken to a serving dish and keep warm.

Bring juices to a boil in the roasting pan with the orange peel and orange juice, blending to incorporate any browned particles. Remove from heat and stir in 1 more tablespoon butter until melted, then pour juices into a serving container.

Spoon hot peas around chicken and garnish with sliced, peeled oranges. Set a cluster of bay leaves on the chicken.

Heat liqueur quickly until just slightly warm to touch, set afire, and pour over the chicken. Carve and serve, passing the pan juices to spoon onto each portion. Makes 5 to 6 servings.

Roast Chicken

Green Salad with Mint and Bacon (page 24) goes nicely with this chicken.

5 to 6-pound roasting chicken
  Salt
1 clove garlic, minced or mashed
⅛ teaspoon pepper
1 teaspoon marjoram leaves
2 tablespoons lemon juice
3 tablespoons Madeira

Sprinkle chicken inside and out lightly with salt and set on a rack in a roasting pan, breast up, with wings tucked under the back; do not truss. Blend garlic, pepper, marjoram, and lemon juice and brush over the chicken.

Bake chicken in a 350° oven for about 1 hour and 45 minutes to 2 hours or until the thigh joint wiggles easily.

Drain juices from cooked chicken cavity into roasting pan, then transfer chicken to a serving dish and keep warm. Skim fat from pan juices and add Madeira to pan; bring to a boil, scraping free browned bits. Serve in a small bowl. Spoon over portions of the carved chicken. Makes 5 to 6 servings.

Turkey Cannelloni

For making a grand splash, here is an involved, large scale entrée that is suitable for very special occasions. It makes 40 servings.

You can divide the chores into these steps: (1) roast turkey; (2) make filling; (3) cook pancakes; (4) make tomato sauce; (5) prepare cream sauce; (6) slice cheese; (7) assemble; (8) bake and serve.

Since cannelloni are rather rich, salad and bread are all you need to complete a main course. A simple dessert such as fruit and an uniced cake or sweet bread would be appropriate.

12 to 14-pound turkey (including giblets), roasted and cooled, with drippings
2 pound slice center cut cooked ham, bone removed
2 pounds (1 qt.) cottage cheese
2 cups shredded Parmesan cheese
6 eggs, beaten
½ teaspoon ground nutmeg
4 teaspoons salt

Cream sauce:

¾ cup (⅜ lb.) butter or margarine
1 cup unsifted all-purpose flour
3 quarts milk
2 cups canned or freshly made chicken broth or turkey broth
1½ teaspoons salt
  Tomato sauce (recipe follows)
  Thin pancakes (recipe follows)
4 pounds jack cheese, thinly sliced

Peel skin from cooked turkey and strip all meat from carcass. (If you like, save skin and bones to make broth for soups.) Skim fat from drippings and reserve drippings.

Cut turkey pieces and ham into small chunks. Grind through the fine blade of a food chopper the turkey, ham, cottage cheese, and Parmesan cheese. Mix the turkey drippings and eggs thoroughly with the ground meats and cheeses. Season meat with nutmeg and salt. Chill, covered, until ready to use (overnight if convenient). Makes about 20 cups.

In a kettle (about 6-qt. size) melt butter and blend in flour for the cream sauce, stirring until lightly browned. Gradually stir in the milk and broth and add the salt. Bring mixture to a boil, stirring frequently, and simmer slowly for about 20 minutes. Add the tomato sauce and simmer 5 or 10 minutes longer. Cool and chill, covered, until ready to use (overnight if you wish).

To assemble, spoon ¼ cup of the ground meat filling along the center of each pancake and roll pancake around filling. Repeat this process until all meat is used. Place pancakes seam side down, side by side, in shallow baking pans (you will need 4 pans, each 11 by 17 inches or ones with equivalent areas). Ladle the cream sauce mixture evenly over the filled pancakes. Top pancakes with slices jack cheese.

Bake in a 400° oven for 20 to 25 minutes or until the cheese is melted and the sauce is bubbling. Use a wide spatula to lift the pancakes onto dinner plates. Allow 2 filled pancakes for each serving. Makes about 80 pancakes or 40 servings.

Tomato sauce: Melt 4 tablespoons (⅛ lb.) butter or margarine in a saucepan. Add 2 large chopped onions and cook until soft. Stir in 1 large can (1 lb. 12 oz.) whole tomatoes, breaking the tomatoes into large chunks. Season with 2 teaspoons basil leaves and ½ teaspoon salt, and simmer, uncovered, for 15 minutes. Add, hot or cooled, to cream sauce.

Thin pancakes: Beat together until smooth 6⅔ cups milk, 3⅓ cups unsifted all-purpose flour, 16 eggs, and 2½ teaspoons salt. For each pancake, melt about ½ teaspoon butter or margarine (you'll need about 1 cup total) in a 7 or 8-inch frying pan. Add about 2 tablespoons of the batter and tilt quickly to coat bottom of pan. Cook until brown; turn and cook other side. Repeat for each pancake until all batter is used. Cool pancakes and stack; package airtight. You can store them a day or two in the refrigerator or freeze; thaw completely and bring to room temperature before attempting to separate. Makes 80 to 90 pancakes.

Turkey Tarragon Scallopini

The next two recipes each use about 1½ pounds boneless turkey breast. Sometimes you can buy turkey breast fresh and by weight, but if your only choice is to purchase a whole frozen breast, ask your meatman to saw it into smaller sections of this size. Wrap remaining sections individually and store in the freezer for later use.

> About 1½ pounds boneless turkey breast, thawed if frozen
> ¼ cup all-purpose flour
> About 5 tablespoons butter or margarine
> ¼ pound mushrooms, sliced
> 1 tablespoon finely chopped parsley
> ½ teaspoon each salt and tarragon leaves, crumbled
> ⅛ teaspoon pepper
> ⅓ cup dry Vermouth

Slice turkey across the grain into ½-inch-thick slices; lay the slices between waxed paper and pound with a flat surfaced mallet until slices are uniformly ¼ inch thick. Pound evenly and gently to avoid tearing meat, replacing paper as needed. Dredge pieces of meat in flour, coating all over; shake off excess flour.

Melt about half the butter in a large frying pan over medium high heat; add turkey slices without crowding and cook until just lightly browned on each side; takes about 4 minutes total. As pieces are cooked, transfer to a serving dish and cover to keep warm.

Melt remaining butter in pan, reduce heat to medium, add mushrooms, and cook until they are limp, about 5 minutes. Stir in parsley, salt, tarragon, pepper, and Vermouth; boil for about 2 minutes, stirring to incorporate brown bits clinging to pan. Pour evenly over turkey and serve. Makes 4 to 6 servings.

Turkey La Scala

> About 1½ pounds boneless turkey breast, thawed if frozen
> ¼ cup all-purpose flour
> 2 tablespoons each olive oil and butter or margarine
> 1 egg beaten with 2 tablespoons water
> 1 package (10 oz.) frozen petite (or tiny) peas, thawed
> 2 ounces very thinly sliced prosciutto
> ¾ pound (12 oz.) teleme cheese, thinly sliced
> ⅛ teaspoon each ground nutmeg and pepper

Slice turkey across the grain into ½-inch-thick slices; lay slices between waxed paper and pound gently and evenly with a flat surfaced mallet until slices are uniformly ¼ inch thick, changing waxed paper as needed.

Dredge pieces of meat in flour, coating all over; shake off excess flour. In a large frying pan, start heating together the olive oil and butter over medium-high heat. Dip turkey slices, one at a time, in the egg-water mixture to coat thoroughly; drain briefly and then slip each piece into frying pan (don't crowd pieces in pan). Sauté, turning once, until lightly browned on both sides, about 3 minutes total; remove cooked turkey and drain briefly.

Arrange cooked turkey, overlapping as needed, in a shallow baking dish (about 8 by 12 inches). Spoon peas evenly around turkey. Arrange prosciutto evenly over turkey; finish with an even layer of teleme cheese overall. Cover dish (you can refrigerate it at this point up to 24 hours, if you like). Bake in a 400° oven for 20 minutes (35 minutes if refrigerated) or until cheese melts. Sprinkle with nutmeg and pepper and serve. Makes 6 servings.

Fish, Cheese, & Eggs

Sole Roman style, cioppino, fonduta,
frittatas to serve anytime

Rather than investigating the great many Italian dishes based on fish, cheese, and eggs, this chapter just samples some of the good things that can be encountered in Italy or that have been created by Italian-American cooks.

The Mediterranean and Adriatic Seas provide the Italian cook with fish and shellfish, many of which have international counterparts. These recipes use fish available in this country.

Steamed Clams with Rice

Serve the clams and liquid in wide, rimmed bowls and add rice. The rice and broth make a delicious soup accompaniment for the clams.

4 tablespoons butter or margarine
4 tablespoons finely chopped parsley
1 or 2 cloves garlic, minced or mashed
2 cups regular strength chicken broth
1 cup dry white wine (or ¼ cup lemon juice
    with ¾ cup regular strength chicken
    broth)
3 dozen small hard-shell clams, washed well
1 to 2 cups hot, cooked rice

Heat the butter in a large, heavy kettle. Add the parsley and garlic and sauté 1 to 2 minutes. Pour in the chicken broth and wine and bring to a boil. Add the clams, cover, and simmer gently until clams open, about 5 to 10 minutes.

To serve, spoon some of the hot rice into each large soup bowl or soup plate. Arrange opened clams in each bowl, then pour over the broth and serve immediately. Makes about 4 servings.

Roman Style Oven Fried Sole

Preparing sole in the remarkably easy Roman way eliminates problems of overbrowning and uneven cooking that occur when a whole sole is sautéed in a frying pan; less fat is also required.

Five kinds of sole (of the flounder family in Pacific coastal waters) are of the right size to cook and serve whole; English, Dover, rex, sand dab, and petrale. Curlfin turbot and sand sole are also suitable.

You will need oven-proof dishes, such as individual steak plates (for individual servings) or a large platter for several servings. The hot dish will keep the fish warm while you bone it for serving.

1 to 1¼ pounds whole sole, head and entrails
    removed (dressed weight is 3/4 to 1 lb.)
    or 2 small whole sole (6 to 12 oz. size),
    head and entrails removed, for each
    serving
    Water
    Salt and pepper or lemon pepper
    All-purpose flour
2 tablespoons butter (or 1 tablespoon each
    butter and olive oil) for each fish

Rinse fish with cold water and pat dry. Have a heat-proof metal or ceramic plate ready into which the fish will fit alone or side by side without overlapping. (You can use several large platters in one oven.) Set the plate or plates in the oven to preheat; 500° if metal, 450° if glass or ceramic.

Sprinkle fish with salt and pepper or the lemon pepper. Then coat fish with flour and shake off excess.

Remove hot platters from oven and add 2 tablespoons butter for each fish that will go into this container, swirling until butter is melted. Turn fish in butter to coat both sides. Immediately return to the oven and bake until fish browns and flakes easily when prodded with a fork; it takes 8 to 10 minutes for the large fish and 4 to 6 minutes for the small fish. Bring the hot plates to the table and set on insulated mats or wooden plate liners. Have ready two serving tools such as a spoon and a pie server or two spoons; also have a plate for bones. Remove bones from fish as directed below.

Baccalá con Morselata

An Old World staple with undeniably assertive character is dried salt cod. This hard, flat fish—treated with respect and imagination in cuisines all around the Mediterranean—is found in stores that specialize in foods from Italy, Portugal, Greece, Spain, or Mexico.

If you enjoy plain, peasant-style dishes, a liking for this robustly flavored preparation of baccalá will come easily. The flavor of the fish is rather mild (surprising after the pungent cooking aroma) and the texture is coarse and chewy.

The fish soaks and freshens in water for 1 to 2 days before cooking.

About 2 pounds (1 average-sized) salt cod
Water
¾ cup olive oil
2 bunches (or about 2 lbs.) Swiss chard, well washed and drained
2 large onions, chopped
8 leeks, thinly sliced (include tender green part)
½ small head cabbage, coarsely chopped
1½ cups dry white wine
1 can (about 1 lb.) whole or pear-shaped Italian style tomatoes
3 cans (8 oz. each) tomato sauce
1 can (about 14 oz.) regular strength chicken broth
Hot cooked polenta (see page 41, make the full recipe and spoon out portions to serve, or mold and slice)

How to Bone Sole

1. Find the line along edge of fish where row of fine lateral fin bones stops; cut and separate bony edges from the sole.

2. Repeat on other edge of sole to cut away the fine fin bones. With spoon and server, remove the bony edges from plate.

3. Cut along the center crease that marks the vertebral column to separate the two boneless sections on top side of the sole.

4. Working from center, lift and push fillets away from bones to sides of plate. Cut off tail (leave in place, if you wish).

5. Grasp bone firmly at one end with serving tools or a finger and lift, exposing boneless underside of sole; discard bones.

6. For attractive presentation, you can reassemble fish, moving pieces from sides of plate back in place on top of the fish.

Wash the cod under cold running water, then immerse in cold water (cut in pieces, if necessary, to fit into a container); cover and keep cold 24 to 48 hours. Change water 2 to 3 times during this period. Immerse cod in boiling water to cover, and simmer, uncovered, for 15 minutes. Drain and cover with cold water. When cool enough to touch, remove and discard all bones, skin, and cartilage. Keep the cod cold, covered, until ready to use.

In a large deep kettle heat the oil. Chop the chard and reserve 2 cups of the green tops. Add the rest of the chard, onions, leeks, and cabbage to oil. Cook, stirring, over high heat until vegetables are soft.

Blend in wine, tomatoes (break up with a spoon) and liquid, tomato sauce, and chicken broth. Bring to a boil, cover, and simmer 1½ to 2 hours; stir occasionally. (Chill sauce, covered, if made ahead, then reheat to use.) Add cooked cod to sauce. Cover and simmer gently 1 more hour; stir occasionally.

Immerse reserved chard greens in boiling salted water and cook over high heat, uncovered, for 5 minutes. Drain well and stir into cod mixture.

Ladle into wide bowls over hot polenta. Makes 8 to 10 servings.

Stuffed Clam Appetizer

Patterned after baked clams served in Naples, this appetizer makes an interesting way to begin a meal.

2 dozen small hard-shell clams, well
    scrubbed
2 tablespoons water
¼ cup (⅛ lb.) butter or margarine
1 large clove garlic, minced or mashed
2 tablespooons finely chopped parsley
3 tablespoons fresh bread crumbs (whirl
    about ½ slice bread in a covered
    blender) or 1 tablespoon fine dry bread
    crumbs

Put clams in a large kettle with the water; cook over moderate heat, covered, just until the shells open. Remove from heat, and when cool enough to handle, pluck the whole clams from the shells; save half the shells.

Blend together the butter, garlic, parsley, and bread crumbs. Set each clam back into a half shell and spread with about 1 teaspoon of the butter mixture. Arrange filled shells side by side in a shallow baking pan. (You can do this much ahead; cover and refrigerate until time to serve.)

Broil clams 4 inches from heat source until lightly browned; takes 3 to 4 minutes. Makes 2 dozen appetizers.

Cioppino

A soupy fish stew, cioppino, was probably dreamed up in San Francisco, and more than likely by an Italian. You can make it in many ways, but you'll always start with delicious Pacific Dungeness crab. Cioppino can be quite robustly seasoned, or it can also be lightly seasoned (as this one is) to emphasize the delicate flavor of the crab.

Cook crab and shrimp in their shells for an authentic taste. Since the stew is rather messy to eat, have plenty of napkins available. Green salad and bread complete the meal.

¾ cup (⅜ lb.) butter or margarine
2 medium-sized onions, chopped
2 or 3 whole garlic cloves
1 cup packed chopped parsley (about 1
    bunch)
2 large cans (1 lb. 12 oz. each) whole
    tomatoes
2 cans (about 14 oz. each) regular strength
    chicken broth
1 bay leaf
1 tablespoon basil leaves
½ teaspoon each thyme leaves and oregano
    leaves
1 cup water
1½ cups dry white wine
1½ pounds large shrimp (or boneless,
    skinless, chunks of rock fish or ling cod)
2 large Dungeness crab, live, cleaned, and
    cracked (have your fishman do this for
    you)
1½ pounds scallops

Melt the butter in a large kettle and add onions, garlic, and parsley; cook, stirring, until onion is soft. Add the tomatoes (breaking into chunks) and liquid, broth, bay, basil, thyme, oregano, water, and wine. Cover and simmer for about 30 minutes.

Devein the shrimp in this manner: insert a small metal or wooden skewer along the back of each shrimp (in shell) beneath the vein. Gently pull the skewer to surface, drawing out vein as you do so; repeat as often as necessary to remove the entire vein. Set shrimp aside.

Add crab to the simmering sauce and cook, covered, for 10 minutes. Then add the shrimp and scallops and return stew to boiling, then cover and simmer 5 to 7 minutes more or until scallops are opaque throughout.

Serve stew from the kettle or a tureen into large soup bowls; have a large bowl available to hold shells as they are emptied. Makes 8 to 10 servings.
Note: If you can not get live Dungeness crab, use cooked, cleaned, cracked crab and add it to the sauce when you add the shrimp.

Fried Squid

Squid or inkfish may be found fresh or frozen in fish markets, in Italian or Oriental food markets, and is increasingly available frozen in supermarkets.

Fried squid is equal to abalone for tenderness and delicacy of flavor.

1 to 2 pounds fresh or thawed, frozen squid
  Garlic-flavored salt
  Equal portions fine dry bread crumbs and all-purpose flour (about 1 cup total for 1 lb. squid)

To clean each squid (see below) hold under running water and pull off and discard the speckled membrane that covers the mantle or hood. Pull the transparent shell or sword out from inside the hood and discard it. Pull the body from the hood; strip off and discard the material that easily separates from the body (including the ink sac). Squeeze out and discard contents of the hood, and rinse hood inside. Pop out parrot-like beak from between the legs. Slice mantle crosswise in ¼ to ½-inch-wide strips, forming rings. Drain squid, then sprinkle with garlic-flavored salt. Coat squid with mixture of crumbs and flour; shake off excess.

In a medium-sized, deep saucepan, heat 1½ inches salad oil to 375°. Cook rings a spoonful at a time for about 30 seconds or until lightly browned; *squid gets excessively tough if overcooked.*

Drain rings, keeping warm. Bring oil back to 375° before each addition. Cook squid bodies with legs last, also for about 30 seconds; they tend to spatter fat so have a lid handy to cover pan loosely. Serve at once.

One pound of squid makes 2 or 3 main dish servings or 6 appetizer servings.

Insalata di Mare

Scoglio di Frisio, a Roman restaurant specializing in Neapolitan dishes, offers this lemony fragrant squid salad as a first course.

  Water
1 pound fresh or frozen, thawed squid, cleaned as directed for Fried Squid
1 can (10 oz.) whole clams
  Peel of 1 small lemon (pared thinly with a vegetable peeler), cut in very thin strips
4 tablespoons lemon juice
⅓ cup olive oil
2 tablespoons minced parsley
  Salt and pepper

Bring a quantity of water to boil over high heat. Drop in squid and cook just until edges begin to curl, about when boiling resumes. Drain and set aside.

Drain liquid from clams into a saucepan. Add lemon peel and bring to a boil; remove from heat and stir in clams and cooked squid; chill, covered.

How to Clean Squid

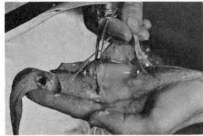

1. Pull speckled membrane from hood exposing pure white meat.

2. Pull the sword or shell (hence, squid is a shellfish) from inside of the hood.

3. Separate body from hood by gently drawing apart. Rinse out hood.

4. Pop out horny beak mouth; squid has eight tentacled legs, two arms.

5. Cut the hood or mantle crosswise in ¼ to ½-inch strips to make rings.

6. Squid rings and body curlicues are fried. Overcooking toughens squid.

Stir in the lemon juice, olive oil, parsley, salt and pepper to taste. Serve cool, but not ice cold. Makes 6 first course servings.

Mascarpone

Mascarpone, fresh cheese made from thick, rich cream, is used in many ways: spread on bread, whipped and made into desserts, or flavored to go with fruits. This recipe is an approximation of the flavor and texture of mascarpone.

    1   large package (8 oz.) cream cheese, at
            room temperature
    ¼   cup unsifted powdered sugar
    2   tablespoons half-and-half
    2   tablespoons Cointreau or other
            orange-flavored liqueur (or 1 tablespoon
            thawed frozen orange juice concentrate)
        Apricot halves

Beat the cheese with sugar, cream, and Cointreau until smoothly blended. Mound on a serving plate and swirl into an attractive cone. Surround with apricot halves. Spread mascarpone onto fruit to eat. Makes 4 to 6 dessert servings.

Fonduta

Both the wonderfully fragrant white truffles and the fontina cheese that make up this classic Italian version of a Swiss cheese fondue come from the Piedmont region of Northern Italy.

Fonduta may be served in the same manner as cheese fondue, with bite-sized chunks of crusty bread swirled through the smooth sauce. But it is also a superb sauce spooned onto sautéed or grilled veal—a popular practice in Turin. Similar dishes are typical in Bologna, too.

    8   ounces fontina or fontinella cheese,
            shredded (or 6 oz. mozzarella and 2 oz.
            Bel Paese cheeses)
    ½   cup plus about 4 tablespoons half-and-half
    1   teaspoon all-purpose flour
        Dash white pepper
    3   egg yolks, slightly beaten
    1   can (1 oz.) white truffles (optional)
    1   tablespoon butter, cut in small pieces
        French bread, cut in cubes, or bread sticks

Place cheese in shallow bowl; stir in the ½ cup half-and-half. Cover and let stand for 30 minutes. Mean-

White Truffles...
An Olfactory Sensation

An American attempting to describe the appearance of the culinary jewel of Alba, the white truffle, invariably compares it to a potato. Curiously, when the potato was made known to the continent after its discovery in the New World, it was the Italians who likened it to the white truffle. It is with appearance that the similarity of these two products from beneath the soil ends. The white truffle, a lesser known member of the fungus family to which the black truffles of France belong, is distinguished by the incredibly pervasive, unique aroma that it emanates. It complements exquisitely the flavors of such foods as cheese, eggs, creamy sauces, and delicate meats. When the fall harvest is in full sway, the Italians use them with abandon in their finest dishes, such as Fonduta (this page), slivering the raw truffle into crisp, thin brown flakes (see truffle slicer page 6). Rarely, a fine food merchant in this country will fly in a few specimens for favored clientele; but ordinarily, you will need to search them out canned in fancy food shops dealing in Italian imports. White truffles are costly, but you may find the extravagance worthwhile for special occasions.

while, blend flour and pepper with egg yolks. Drain liquid from the truffles and measure. Add enough half-and-half to truffle liquid to make ¼ cup total. (If truffles are omitted, use 4 tablespoons half-and-half.)

Blend liquid into egg yolk mixture. Slice truffles paper thin with a truffle slicer, a vegetable peeler, or a very sharp knife. Blend egg yolk mixture into cheese.

Cook in the top of a double boiler over gently boiling water (water should not touch underside of upper portion of the double boiler), stirring constantly, until cheese melts and mixture is just thickened and smooth. Stir in butter until melted. (If made ahead, warm slowly over hot, not boiling, water, stirring frequently.)

Place in chafing dish over warm water to serve. Dunk bread cubes on fondue forks or bamboo skewers, or use bread sticks to dip up the mixture. Makes 3 to 4 main dish servings.

Ricotta Pancakes

Brought to our attention by an Italian-American cook, these fine-textured, tender pancakes make a delightful high protein dessert or brunch entrée. You can make them ahead and reheat to serve.

1 cup (½ lb.) ricotta cheese
3 eggs
2 tablespoons salad oil
¼ cup unsifted all-purpose flour
2 teaspoons sugar
¼ teaspoon salt
About 2 cups fresh or frozen raspberries
Soft butter or margarine
Powdered sugar

In a blender jar combine ricotta, eggs, salad oil, flour, sugar, and salt. Cover and whirl until smooth; push ingredients from sides of blender with a rubber spatula. (Or rub ricotta through a wire strainer, then beat with remaining ingredients until mixture is smoothly blended.)

Pour batter in about 3-inch rounds on a lightly greased griddle or wide frying pan over medium-low heat. Turn cakes with a spatula when bubbles form on the surface. When browned lightly on both sides, remove from pan. Keep warm until all are cooked. (To make ahead, cool pancakes on wire racks; then to reheat, place in a single layer on a baking sheet. Cover and bake for 5 minutes in a 375° oven.)

Serve pancakes hot and accompany with raspberries. If you like, serve with butter and a liberal dusting of powdered sugar. Makes about 15 pancakes; or 3 entrée servings or 5 dessert servings.

Tomatoes and Eggs with Mushrooms

For a brunch, begin this meal with fresh figs and sliced coppa, then serve the eggs with thick slices of buttered, toasted French bread. Finish with strong hot coffee blended with hot milk.

3 or 4 large tomatoes, peeled
1 pound mushrooms, thinly sliced
3 tablespoons butter or olive oil
6 to 8 eggs
   Salt and pepper
¾ cup shredded jack cheese

Cut tomatoes in cubes and drain in a colander for several minutes. Meanwhile, in a 10 to 11-inch frying pan, cook mushrooms in butter over high heat, stirring, until they are limp and juices have evaporated. Add tomatoes and stir to heat through. With a spoon make 6 or 8 nest spaces and break an egg into each space. Sprinkle with salt and pepper and cover evenly with the cheese. Cover pan and cook on low heat until eggs are set as you like. Makes 3 to 4 servings.

Spinach and Asparagus Frittata

A frittata is a mixture of eggs and vegetables rather like an omelet, except that it is cooked on both sides in a wide frying pan. It is served flat, cut in sections for individual portions, and eaten hot or cool as a luncheon main dish with salad or sliced tomatoes, or alone as a light snack. You need a non-stick fluorocarbon finish pan, a well seasoned cast-iron pan, or any other type of frying pan that is not inclined to stick.

1 pound spinach, stems discarded and leaves washed and drained
1 pound asparagus, tough ends discarded and stems cut in 1-inch lengths
   Boiling salted water
8 eggs
3 tablespoons whipping cream or water
¼ teaspoon salt
   Pepper
2 tablespoons shredded Parmesan or Romano cheese
4 tablespoons olive oil
2 cloves garlic, minced or mashed

Place spinach in a covered pan and cook over medium heat until wilted, stirring occasionally; about 2 minutes. Pour into a colander and let drain; when cool, coarsely chop.

Cook asparagus in about ½ inch boiling salted water in a wide frying pan just until tender to pierce; about 3 minutes. Drain and immerse in cold water to cool quickly (this preserves the green color of the asparagus), then drain again.

Beat eggs, cream, salt, a dash of pepper, and cheese just enough to evenly blend whites and yolks; set aside.

In a 10 to 11-inch frying pan (one in which foods do not stick) combine 3 tablespoons of the oil and the garlic. Cook, stirring, over medium heat until garlic is golden; *do not scorch*. Add spinach and asparagus, distributing them evenly in pan; cook about 2 minutes to heat through. Pour egg mixture over vegetables and cook, without stirring, until set about ¼ inch around outer edge. With a wide spatula, lift some of the egg mixture from sides of the pan, all the way around, tipping pan to let uncooked egg flow to pan bottom. Continue cooking until top of frittata is almost set; top ⅛ inch of egg mixture towards center should still be liquid.

Invert a large round flat plate (somewhat wider than frying pan) over frying pan. Holding together, turn frittata out onto plate. Add the remaining 1 tablespoon oil to the frying pan, then slide frittata from plate back into frying pan. Cook about 2 minutes longer to lightly brown bottom, then invert frittata, in the same manner as before, onto a serving plate. Cut in wedges and serve hot or at room temperature. Makes 3 to 4 servings.

Zucchini Frittata:

Follow the recipe for Spinach and Asparagus Frittata, making these changes: omit spinach and asparagus. Cook 1 pound fresh zucchini, thinly sliced, in about ½ inch boiling salted water, covered, until just tender, about 5 minutes. Pour into colander, cool in cold running water; drain. Combine squash; 1 can (2 oz.) sliced, pitted, ripe olives, drained; ½ cup sliced green onion (including part of the tops); and ¼ teaspoon oregano leaves. Add these vegetables to olive oil and garlic, distributing evenly in pan; cook about 2 minutes. Add egg mixture; cook as directed.

Spinach and Ricotta Pie

Try this main dish pie for a family meal, along with a salad and yellow crookneck squash.

1 package (10 to 12 oz.) thawed, frozen chopped spinach
2 cups (1 lb.) ricotta cheese
¼ pound mushrooms, chopped
½ cup each shredded Swiss and Parmesan cheeses
¼ pound thinly sliced pepperoni sausage
¼ cup finely chopped onion
2 teaspoons prepared mustard
½ teaspoon oregano leaves
¼ teaspoon salt
Dash pepper
1 egg, slightly beaten
Pastry for a 2-crust 9-inch pie
Tomato sauce (recipe follows)

Drain spinach thoroughly; press out as much moisture as possible. Blend with ricotta, mushrooms, Swiss and Parmesan cheeses, pepperoni, onion, mustard, oregano, salt, and pepper; stir in egg. Roll out half of the pastry and use to line a 9-inch pie pan. Spread filling in pastry. Roll out remaining pastry for top crust; place on filling, trim and flute edge, pricking top with a fork. Bake in a 425° oven for about 25 minutes, or until crust is browned. Serve hot with tomato sauce. Makes 4 to 6 servings.

Tomato sauce: Heat 1 large can (15 oz.) tomato sauce with ½ teaspoon garlic salt, dash pepper, and 1 teaspoon Italian herb seasoning.

Tosta Party

This quickly managed party, ideal for impromptu festivities, is spirited right from the streets of Milan, where tosta grills abound. Tostas are grilled ham and cheese sandwiches, with savory condiments tucked into them.

In keeping with the informality of such a gathering, let each person cook his own tosta. Serve a green salad, chilled apple juice and white wine; pour beverages separately or blend to make a punch. Finish with fresh fruit.

Tostas

For 6 servings allow ½ to ¾ pound of sliced fontina or tybo cheese, chunk teleme or jack cheese (cut portions as needed), and sliced cooked ham; ¼ to ⅓ pound thinly sliced prosciutto; 1 large loaf (1 lb.) sliced egg bread, Italian or French bread; and the condiments that follow.

If you have an electric sandwich grill, group the elements for the sandwiches alongside. If you cook the tostas in a frying pan, assemble the ingredients in the kitchen.

To make a tosta, place a slice or two of meat and cheese between slices of bread. Toast in a sandwich grill on medium or high heat (or in a frying pan with a lid—even an electric frying pan—on medium heat, turning as needed) until browned and cheese melts; *use no fat.* Open sandwich and add any or all of the condiments. Serve tostas on plates.

Tosta Condiments

Russian dressing: Blend ⅔ cup mayonnaise with ¼ cup drained sweet pickle relish and 2 tablespoons tomato-based chile sauce; keep cold and covered until time to serve.

Canned liver pâté: Open 1 can (about 4¾ oz.) liver pâté.

Red peppers: Seed and sliver 1 large red bell pepper. Cook, covered, over moderately high heat with 2 tablespoons each olive oil and water until liquid evaporates. Remove cover and stir in 1 tablespoon wine vinegar and salt to taste. Serve at room temperature. (Or buy 1 jar—about 8 oz.—sweet fried pepper with onions.)

Onions: Peel 1 large onion and cut vertically in slivers. Place in a wide frying pan with ¼ cup water and 2 tablespoons white wine vinegar; boil and stir until liquid evaporates and onions are limp. Salt to taste and serve at room temperature. (Or buy 1 jar—about 6 oz.—pickled onions and slice thinly.)

Mushrooms: Thinly slice ½ pound mushrooms and sauté in 2 tablespoons olive oil until limp; add 2 tablespoons vinegar and cook until liquid evaporates. Salt to taste and serve at room temperature. (Or buy 1 jar—about 5 oz.—marinated mushrooms and thinly slice.)

Artichokes: Open 2 jars (each 6 oz.) marinated artichoke hearts and cut in thin slices; serve at room temperature.

Eggplant caponata: Open 1 can (about 5 oz.) eggplant caponata and serve.

Pickled peppers: Open 1 jar (about 8 oz.) Italian-style pickled peppers (peperoncini) and serve.

Breads Plain & Sweet

Loaves, pizzas, bread sticks, holiday specials

No Italian meal is complete without bread in some form on the table—big, country style crusty loaves; imaginatively slashed and twisted rolls; thin or fat, short or long bread sticks; pizza; focaccia; to name a few. Then for an afternoon or late evening refreshment, the perfect offering is a slice of a special sweet bread with a glass of sweet, dry, or sparkling wine, or a cup of espresso. This chapter explores these breads in variety.

Adobe Oven Bread

For those of you who do not live where you can buy good Italian or French bread, we include the directions for making an adobe oven in which you can bake this bread successfully. Additionally, the oven is also perfect for making authentic pizza.

- 1 package active dry yeast
- 4 teaspoons sugar
- 4 cups warm water (about 110°)
- 11 to 12 cups unsifted all-purpose flour
- 1 tablespoon salt
- 1 egg beaten well with 4 tablespoons water
  Water

In a large bowl stir yeast and sugar into the 4 cups water; let stand until yeast is dissolved. With a heavy spoon beat in 10 cups of the flour and salt, then turn dough out onto a board coated with 1 more cup of the flour. Pat some of the flour over the dough (it is sticky), then knead for about 10 minutes or until dough is smooth and feels velvety; add more flour to board as required.

Wash the bowl, dry, and rub generously with salad oil; turn dough over in a bowl and cover with clear plastic film. Set in a warm place to rise for about 1 hour 15 minutes, or until doubled in bulk.

Divide dough into pieces of equal size, making 2 to 8 portions. Shape each piece by kneading into a smooth ball; then, if you like, form an oval, round, or long loaf.

Place loaves well apart on floured muslin cloth on baking sheets; dust lightly with flour and cover with cloth. Let loaves rise 30 to 40 minutes, or until puffy-looking. (Refrigerate briefly if loaves rise before correct adobe oven temperature is reached.)

When the preheated adobe oven (see 71) has cooled to about 350°, prepare to transfer the loaves (1 or 2 at a time) onto a floured bread paddle in this manner: lift cloth to roll a loaf slightly onto your palm, then slip bread paddle under loaf and roll it onto the paddle. Slash the top of each loaf in several places with a very sharp knife or razor blade, then brush surface with egg mixture; take care not to let egg run onto board. (To improvise a bread paddle, secure a steady handle to a smooth, thin board large enough to hold at least 1 loaf.)

When the preheated adobe oven has cooled to between 325° and 300°, slip the loaves onto the clean oven floor; if you can, load from front to back (the back is hottest). Work quickly, and when all loaves are in the oven, set door in place. Check temperature in 5 minutes; if above 400°, remove door until oven temperature drops to 350°, then close. After a total of 10 minutes, squirt loaves all over with water forced from a turkey baster or a sprayer. Close door, and after 10 minutes, squirt loaves with water again.

Close door and continue baking about 40 to 60 minutes, depending on size of loaves and oven temperature, until loaves are a rich golden brown. Pull out onto oven hearth to cool; serve while still slightly warm to touch or when cooled completely. Break or slice loaves. Makes 2 large or 8 small loaves.

Italian Sausage Pizza

Pizza is considered either a preliminary course for a meal or an entrée, depending upon the size portion you elect to serve. You can use a conventional oven or the adobe oven to bake any of the following pizzas. Basic instructions for using the adobe oven are included in this recipe. Sausage tops this pizza, but you can also use any favorite pizza topping.

1 package active dry yeast
1 cup warm water
½ teaspoon salt
2 teaspoons olive oil
  About 3½ cups unsifted all-purpose flour
  Olive oil
  Tomato sauce (recipe follows)
  Cooked sausage (directions follow)
¾ pound mozzarella cheese, shredded
  Cornmeal

Soften yeast in water; stir in salt and the 2 teaspoons olive oil. Gradually mix in 3 cups of the flour to form a soft dough. Turn dough onto a board coated with about ½ cup flour and knead until smooth and elastic, about 5 minutes. Place in a greased bowl; turn dough over to grease top. Cover and let rise in a warm place until doubled in bulk, about 1 hour.

Punch down dough and knead on a lightly floured board to shape into a smooth ball. Divide dough in half and roll out each piece on a floured board until about ¾ inch thick. Gently pull each portion into an oval 12 to 14 inches long and 8 to 10 inches wide.

To bake in an adobe oven, assemble the pizzas, one at a time, directly on a cornmeal dusted bread paddle in this manner: brush top of dough generously with olive oil. Spread half of the tomato sauce to within ¾ inch of the rim; top with half the cooked sausage and sprinkle evenly with half the cheese.

Slip pizza from paddle directly onto oven floor when temperature drops to 550°. *Leave door open* and cook about 5 minutes or until pizza is browned; rotate once with the paddle, if needed, to brown edges evenly. To bake more than one pizza, fill the oven from front to back, as the back is the hottest.

When the temperature drops to 450° and if you are still baking pizzas, they will take about 10 minutes to brown; *set the door in place* and check in 5 minutes. If the temperature is over 500°, remove door and let cool to 450° before closing again. You can continue to bake pizzas as the oven cools, but time required for browning will gradually increase.

To bake in a conventional oven, place each oval of dough on a greased baking sheet and brush generously with olive oil. Top with sauce, sausage, and cheese as directed for the pizza baked in the adobe oven. Place one baking sheet at a time on the lowest rack of a 500° oven. Bake 10 to 12 minutes or until crust is browned.

To serve, cut hot pizzas into wedges. Makes 2 large pizzas or 4 main dish servings.

Tomato sauce: Combine 3 cans (1 lb. *each*) Italian style pear-shaped tomatoes (break up tomatoes with spoon), 1 can (6 oz.) tomato paste, 1 teaspoon basil leaves, and ½ teaspoon *each* rosemary leaves and oregano leaves. Boil rapidly, stirring occasionally, until thick and reduced to about 2 cups.

Cooked sausage: Peel and discard casing from 1 pound mild Italian pork sausages; crumble meat into a frying pan and cook, stirring, until lightly browned. With a slotted spoon, lift meat from pan; drain.

Salami Pizza

Frozen bread dough, stretched thin, is the base of this pizza.

You can use salami, or other cold meats such as Lebanon bologna or cooked ham.

½ pound thinly sliced dry salami
2 baked pizza crusts (directions follow)
1 medium-sized mild onion
1¾ pounds mozzarella cheese, sliced or
  shredded
1 teaspoon each basil leaves and oregano
  leaves, crumbled
1 cup freshly shredded Parmesan cheese

Cut salami slices in quarters and distribute over pizza crusts; press down lightly to flatten any bubbles in crusts. Thinly slice onion and separate into rings; scatter over meat. Arrange mozzarella over onions. Sprinkle the basil, oregano, and Parmesan evenly over all.

Bake one pizza at a time in a 500° oven, on the lowest rack position, for 8 to 10 minutes, or until the crust is richly browned and the cheese melts and bubbles. Cut in serving size pieces with scissors. Makes two 12-inch pizzas, 4 main dish servings.

Baked pizza crusts: Thaw 1 loaf (1 lb.) frozen bread dough following package directions and divide dough in half.

Grease two 13-inch pizza pans (or 12 by 15-inch baking sheets) with olive oil. On a lightly floured pastry cloth, roll and stretch each portion of the thawed dough to a 12-inch circle (or 9 by 14-inch rectangle); transfer to pans. Brush olive oil over surface of dough. Bake in 500° oven for 4 minutes or until crusts just begin to brown.

Arrange and level 12 concrete blocks (6 by 8 by 16 inches) in a 32 by 48-inch rectangle. Top with two layers of bricks (you'll need 96). For a more generous hearth (see picture below) add 4 more blocks, set in two layers perpendicular to other blocks, using 16 blocks in all.

Cut drum (see page 71) in half; cut draft hole in drum end to fit 1-pound can; set drum on a wall of bricks stacked 3 high (this takes 33 more, for a total of 129 bricks). Shape over drum a 3 by 4-foot piece of 4-inch concrete wire; tuck excess under drum front. Mold same-sized piece of chicken wire over top and back of drum; cut out draft hole.

Fit can in draft hole, exposing 4 inches. Force blended mud (12 shovels mud with 4 shovels cement plus water) through wire onto drum. Make walls at least 4 inches thick. You need about 3 bags cement.

Put door (2 inches thick, with arched top and handle) in place and mold close-fitting oven opening. Remove door when mud firms slightly. Smooth surface by hand with a little water. Cover with wet cloths, plastic sheet.

When mud has cured 4 or 5 days under wet cloths, uncover and paint with exterior latex. After frequent use, repaint the oven to help conceal heat cracks and smoke marks.

Heat oven with blazing, well fed fire burning for 3 hours or until outside of oven is quite hot to touch; do not pack in wood so tightly that you can not see back of oven.

Scoop out wood and put into fire-proof container, working quickly. Clear corners with a hoe. Have all equipment ready to use.

Sweep oven with a damp broom, then clean with slightly damp mop. Plug draft with wet rags. Work fast. Check temperature with oven thermometer.

Slip raised loaves from floured paddle onto oven floor; fill from front to back (back part is hottest). Set door back in place.

Making an Adobe Oven

This solid, quaint, plastered-earth oven does something that we think justifies a day or two of puttering around in the mud: It bakes fine crusty loaves as much like those you find in Italy, France, and San Francisco as you can ever hope to achieve at home.

And it cooks the rest of the meal, too.

It is typical of primitive ovens in use the world over, although the shapes, sizes, and materials of these ovens vary.

The way the oven works is elemental: You build a fire in it to heat walls and floor, then clean it out and cook in the declining heat.

Illustrated above are steps for the simple, inexpensive way the oven was constructed. It will withstand rain and sun; but should you tire of it, a sledge hammer will break the crust and free the unmortared interior bricks and blocks.

A 28-gallon paper barrel or drum (about 27 inches tall) split lengthwise with hacksaw or saber-saw provides the form for the top contour; later it is simply burned out. Buy a drum from the lumberyard or see the classified telephone directory under "Barrels & Drums."

Two layers of wire mesh (of different weights) hold and reinforce the thick adobe-like exterior (we had good results with the dirt-cement blend using soils ranging from loamy to hard clay).

The oven dries out and cures under frequently moistened wet cloths for about a week before firing.

Expect harmless cracks to develop when it is heated.

Regulating the Heat

A warning: The oven holds intense heat, and can char a loaf or roast in very few minutes if too hot. Trust the readings of a mercury oven thermometer; most cooks who have trouble put the food in the oven before it is cool enough.

Follow the steps shown above to heat and clean the oven, then plug the draft. Set thermometer (one that registers up to 700°) in the middle of the oven where you can easily see it. If the oven is properly heated, the temperature will be near 600°—over or slightly under. Leave oven open to cool; depending on drafts, air temperature, and original heat of oven, it will take 30 to 40 minutes to drop to the bread baking temperature of about 325°.

The most critical timing comes when dough is ready to shape. A team operation works best until you become proficient, as the loaves should be formed just before you clean the oven and the steps may overlap.

A good timetable is to start the fire first; make dough about 1½ hours before you expect the oven to be ready to clear; shape loaves, and at once clear oven to start cooling it. If loaves are ready to bake before oven is cooled, refrigerate; if oven is ready first, close the door.

An Adobe Oven Dinner

To produce a meal of distinction from your adobe oven, follow this routine:

When oven temperature drops to 500°, push a small baking pan with rack holding a 5-pound cross-rib or sirloin tip roast (with meat thermometer in thickest part) to the very back of the oven, but do not close door. Just before oven is ready for the bread (about 350°), put alongside the pan as many as 6 each scrubbed, medium-sized baking potatoes or beets and medium-sized onions in their skins. Put in bread and close the door.

Remove baked bread to hearth to cool; reclose oven and let roast and vegetables continue cooking until meat thermometer registers 135° to 140° (about 45 minutes longer).

Slice roast, peel onions or beets (in Bologna, onions and beets cooked this way are also served cold with an olive oil and wine vinegar dressing), split potatoes, break bread, and apply butter, salt, and pepper as needed. Serve with green salad and wine.

Calzone

Calzone has the same flavors as pizza, but it is made like a huge turnover with the meat, sauce, and melting cheese sealed inside.

It can stand alone as a substantial snack, or, combined with a green salad and soup, it makes an easy supper.

1 can (about 10 oz.) refrigerated parkerhouse rolls
1 can (8 oz.) tomato sauce with onion
1 teaspoon basil leaves
1 teaspoon oregano leaves
2 (about 6 oz.) mild Italian pork sausages
  Water
  About 3 tablespoons olive oil
2¼ cups freshly shredded mozzarella cheese
1½ cups freshly shredded Romano or Parmesan cheese

Open rolls and let stand until they reach room temperature. Heat tomato sauce with basil and oregano; set aside. Simmer sausages in water to cover for 20 minutes; drain, cool, remove the casings, and slice thinly.

For each calzone, compress half the rolls into a flat cake and roll on a floured board to make an 11-inch diameter circle. Brush lightly with oil and spread half the tomato sauce over half the dough circle to within ½-inch of edge. Top sauce with half the sausage; sprinkle with half the mozzarella and Romano cheese.

Fold plain half over filling to within ¼-inch of opposite edge. Roll bottom edge up over top edge; pinch or crimp together to seal. Brush with oil. Repeat to make second calzone. Transfer both calzone with a wide spatula to a greased baking sheet, placing slightly apart. Pierce tops in a few places with a fork. Bake in a 500° oven for 6 minutes, or until golden brown. Makes 2 calzone, or 4 supper servings.

Yeast Focaccia

Focaccia is usually made of yeast dough pressed out flat, then poked full of dents to capture the olive oil and other seasonings that go onto its surface. It's best fresh baked, while still warm and fragrant, to eat as a snack or to go with a meal.

1 loaf (1 lb.) frozen bread dough, thawed
½ cup canned pizza sauce
1 teaspoon garlic salt
¼ cup grated Romano cheese
3 tablespoons olive oil or salad oil

Roll dough out to fit a greased 11 by 15-inch baking pan and place dough in pan. With fingers poke deep holes in dough at 1-inch intervals. Blend pizza sauce with garlic salt and spread evenly over dough. Sprinkle the cheese over the dough and drizzle with the olive oil or salad oil. Let rise in a warm place about 20 minutes, or until almost doubled in bulk. Bake in a 450° oven for 12 to 15 minutes or until edges of crust are well browned. Cut in 2 by 5-inch strips. Serve hot. Makes 14 pieces.

Quick Focaccia

From Genoa comes this easy-to-make version of focaccia; you start with a baking mix and add rubbed sage. It has a biscuit-like texture and a rich herby aroma.

3 cups baking mix (biscuit mix)
2 teaspoons rubbed sage
1 cup milk
6 tablespoons olive oil
  Garlic salt

Blend the baking mix with sage, then stir in milk until evenly mixed. Pour 2 tablespoons of the olive oil in a 9 by 13-inch pan and spread over the bottom. Turn biscuit dough into the pan and pat out, with floured fingers, to make an even layer. Poke holes in dough with fingertips at 1 to 2-inch intervals.

Pour the remaining olive oil evenly over dough, then brush with fingers to coat entire surface. Sprinkle lightly with garlic salt. Bake in a 400° oven for 25 minutes or until richly browned. Cut in rectangles and serve hot or warm. (To recrisp cold focaccia, arrange in a single layer in a pan and place in a 350° oven for about 8 minutes.) Makes 6 to 8 servings.

Fennel Bread Sticks

The same seed that flavors the mild Italian pork sausage makes these crisp bread sticks appealingly aromatic. Served with sweet butter, bread sticks make a delicious appetizer; they are also good with antipasto and soup.

1 package active dry yeast
¾ cup each warm water, salad oil, and beer
1½ teaspoons salt
1 tablespoon fennel seed
4½ cups unsifted all-purpose flour
1 egg beaten with 1 tablespoon water

In a large bowl, soften yeast in the ¾ cup warm water. Add salad oil, beer, salt, and fennel seed. With a wooden spoon, beat in 3½ cups of the flour. On a board or pastry cloth, spread remaining 1 cup flour; turn out soft dough. Knead using this technique: lift edge of the dough, coated well with flour, and fold toward center, avoiding contact with sticky part of dough. Continue folding toward center and kneading, turning the dough as you work, until it is smooth and elastic. Place the dough in a bowl, cover, and let rise until double.

Knead air from dough. Pinch off 1½-inch-diameter lumps and roll each to 18-inch long ropes. Cut each rope in half. Set wire racks on baking sheets and place ropes across them, ½ inch apart. Brush ropes with egg-water mixture. Bake in a 325° oven for about 35 minutes or until evenly browned. Cool, then wrap airtight and store at room temperature. Makes about 7 dozen.

Giant Bread Sticks

Standing tall and toasty crisp all through, these giant bread sticks are a breeze to make.

Pencil thin bread sticks, or grissini, are made in the bustling city of Turin and exported throughout the world. There you find these sticks spectacularly extended to at least a yard in length.

Some Italian bakers in other cities also take the time to make dramatically long bread sticks, though theirs are usually fatter than those of Turin. Long or short, fat or thin, breadsticks are easily made at home.

The maximum length of your bread sticks will be determined by the dimensions of your oven. You can bake the sticks on foil covered oven racks.

    3 to 3½ cups unsifted all-purpose flour
    1 tablespoon sugar
    1 teaspoon salt
    2 packages active dry yeast
    ¼ cup olive oil or salad oil
    1¼ cups hot (120° to 130°) water
    1 egg white beaten with 1 tablespoon water
      Coarse salt, toasted sesame seed, or
      poppy seed (optional)

Put into the large bowl of an electric mixer 1 cup of the flour, the sugar, salt, and yeast; stir to blend. Add the oil. Gradually stir in the hot water, then beat at medium speed for 2 minutes. Add ½ cup more flour, and beat at high speed for 2 minutes. Stir in remaining 1½ to 2 cups flour with your mixer (if it's a heavy-duty model) or a wooden spoon to make a soft dough.

Turn dough out onto a well floured board and, with well floured hands, work it into a smooth ball. Shape dough into an even log or block and, with a sharp knife, cut into 20 equal-sized pieces for 16-inch sticks (or 16 pieces for 20-inch sticks). Roll each piece of dough into a rope that is 16 or 20 inches long, depending on size of pan and oven. Arrange about 1 inch apart on oiled baking sheets or foil-covered racks, rolling to grease all sides of dough.

(If made ahead on pans, cover tightly with clear plastic film and freeze until solid. Then transfer to plastic bags and store in the freezer up to four weeks. Remove frozen sticks from the freezer about 30 minutes before you plan to bake them. Arrange frozen bread sticks on ungreased baking sheet or foil-covered oven rack; cover and let stand at room temperature until fully thawed, about 15 minutes.)

Set dough (unfrozen or thawed) in a warm place, cover, and allow to rise until puffy, about 15 minutes. With a soft brush, paint each stick with the egg white and water. Sprinkle lightly with the salt, sesame seed, or poppy seed, or leave plain. Bake in a 300° oven for about 25 to 30 minutes, or until lightly browned all over. Serve warm or cool. Store airtight or freeze for longer storage. To recrisp baked sticks, put into a 300° oven for about 5 minutes. Makes 16 to 20 extra-long bread sticks.

For appetizer bread sticks, divide the giant bread stick dough into 40 equal pieces. Roll each one to about 12 inches long. Freeze or bake directly on baking sheets or foil-covered oven racks as directed for larger sticks. Bake in a 300° oven for 20 to 25 minutes, or until golden brown. Makes 40 bread sticks.

Pine Nut Sticks

The faintly sweet, resinous flavor of pine nuts becomes more apparent with each bite of these crisp bread sticks.

1 **package yeast, active dry or compressed**
⅔ **cup warm water (lukewarm for compressed yeast)**
½ **teaspoon anise seed, crushed**
2 **tablespoons each salad oil and olive oil**
¼ **teaspoon grated lemon peel**
1 **teaspoon salt**
1 **tablespoon sugar**
  About 2¼ cups unsifted all-purpose flour
⅔ **cup pine nuts (pignoli)**
1 **egg, slightly beaten**
2 **tablespoons coarse salt**

Soften yeast in water; add anise seed, salad oil, olive oil, lemon peel, salt, sugar, and 1 cup of the flour. Beat until smooth. Add pine nuts and enough of the remaining flour to make a stiff dough. Turn out on a floured board and knead until smooth and elastic (about 5 minutes), using additional flour as needed. Place dough in greased bowl, cover with damp cloth, and let rise in warm place until doubled, about 1 hour.

Punch down, divide dough in half. Cut each half into 20 equal-sized pieces; roll each piece, using palms of hands, into a 7-inch length. Place parallel on greased baking sheets about ½ inch apart. Cover and let rise until puffy looking, about 30 minutes; brush with egg, sprinkle lightly with salt. Bake in 325° oven for 30 minutes, until lightly browned. Serve hot or cold. Store airtight at room temperature for 3 to 4 days; freeze for longer storage. Makes 40 bread sticks.

Torta Rustica

This handsome Milanese bread suggests by its very name the ideal setting for its enjoyment: a country picnic. A savory tart, it's also equally good for a patio lunch.

Torta rustica is essentially a baked sandwich; serve it hot, warm, cold, or reheated. Hearty soups or salads are ideal companions. Of the three flavor variations, the spinach and ricotta version goes well with thick minestrone or chicken salad; the sausage and tomato torta is good with split pea soup or Caesar salad; and the tuna and cheese sandwich is complemented by a creamy potato and leek soup with a platter of raw vegetables for munching.

1 **package (13¾ oz.) hot yeast roll mix plus**
  water and egg as specified on the box
1 **filling (3 choices follow)**
  About 2 tablespoons beaten egg

Prepare hot roll mix dough as directed on the package. After the dough has risen, turn onto a lightly floured board and knead to expel air bubbles.

Divide dough in half; roll one portion on floured board into a 9-inch round. Fit dough in bottom of a greased 9 by 1½-inch layer cake pan with removable bottom. Cover evenly with filling.

Shape the remaining portion of the dough in one of the following ways:

Lattice: Roll dough into a 9-inch square and cut in strips about 1 inch wide. Weave the strips over the filling in a lattice pattern, tucking ends of dough down around filling at pan rim.

Wedges: Roll dough into a 9-inch round; cut into 8 pie-shaped wedges. Arrange wedges side by side on filling, with tips meeting in the center.

Circles: Roll dough into a 10-inch round. With a floured 2½-inch doughnut cutter cut 8 or 9 pieces; separate rings and center pieces. Gather scraps and reroll dough into a piece large enough to cut 3 or 4 more rounds, or a total of 10 to 12. Arrange all but one of the rings around the edge of the filling; place remaining ring in the middle, then fit the little round center pieces around the circle in the middle.

Lightly cover the shaped dough and set in a warm place until puffy looking, about 30 to 40 minutes. Uncover and gently brush top with the beaten egg.

Bake on the lowest rack of a 350° oven for 35 to 40 minutes or until bread is richly browned (the spinach and ricotta version is very moist and requires maximum baking time).

Cool bread in pan on a wire rack for about 5 minutes, then remove pan rim. Serve warm, at room temperature, or cool, cover, and refrigerate to serve later. To reheat, wrap chilled bread in foil and bake in a 350° oven for 40 minutes (it takes as long to reheat as to bake). Cut in wedges. Makes 6 to 8 servings.

Spinach and ricotta filling: Wash and drain thoroughly enough fresh spinach leaves to make 1 cup, packed. Force leaves through medium blade of a food chopper (or mince very finely). Blend spinach with 1 cup ricotta cheese, ½ cup shredded Parmesan cheese, 1 egg yolk, ½ teaspoon garlic salt, and ⅛ teaspoon seasoned pepper.

Tuna and cheese filling: Thinly slice 1 small onion, separate into rings, and place in a frying pan with 1 tablespoon olive oil. Add ¼ cup finely chopped red or green pepper and cook, stirring, until onion is lightly browned. Remove from heat and add 1 can (7 oz.) tuna, drained, ½ teaspoon salt, and ¼ teaspoon oregano leaves; stir to break apart tuna. Distribute filling on dough as directed; cover with 1 cup shredded fontina or jack cheese.

Sausage and tomato filling: Remove casing from ¾ pound mild Italian pork sausages and chop the meat coarsely. Cook until browned, stirring; remove from heat and spoon out and discard fat. Blend with meat ¼ cup finely chopped parsley and 2 tablespoons shredded Parmesan cheese. Distribute filling on dough as directed, then top with ½ cup well drained, canned, sliced baby tomatoes and 1 cup shredded mozzarella cheese.

Pane di Ramerino

In the Florentine tradition, this plump round raisin loaf is seasoned with rosemary and olive oil. It is delicious warm, buttered, for brunch, or with salads or soups for lunch. It also makes excellent toast.

¼ cup olive oil
1 teaspoon rosemary leaves
½ cup milk
3 tablespoons sugar
1 teaspoon salt
1 package active dry yeast
¼ cup warm water
2 eggs
　About 3 cups unsifted all-purpose flour
½ cup raisins
　Olive oil
1 tablespoon cold water

Heat the ¼ cup olive oil and the rosemary until hot. Remove from heat and add milk, sugar, and salt;

Panettone Brunch

Sliced Oranges
Grape Clusters
Hot Panettone
Sweet Butter
Fontina Cheese
Hot Cooked Mild Italian Pork
Sausages or Link Pork Sausages
Caffé e Latte

Dust the oranges with powdered sugar. Serve the warm panettone on page 76 or buy a loaf of panettone and warm, wrapped in foil, in a 325° oven for 25 to 30 minutes. Slice and spread with butter and serve with slices of the cheese; accompany with the sausages. Pour equal portions of hot, strong coffee and hot milk into mugs to make caffé e latte.

let stand until lukewarm. Combine yeast with warm water and let stand until softened. Blend yeast, 1 whole egg, 1 egg white, and the oil mixture, then beat in the 3 cups flour. Turn dough onto a floured board and knead about 10 minutes or until smooth and elastic. Flatten dough, top with raisins, and knead lightly to work in raisins (some pop out of dough—just stick them back in).

Rinse mixing bowl and dry, then coat with olive oil. Turn dough over in bowl to grease top, then cover and let rise in a warm place until doubled in bulk; takes 1 to 1½ hours.

Knead dough on floured board again to expel air bubbles, forming a smooth ball. Place on an olive oil coated baking sheet and pat into a flat, 8½-inch diameter round. Brush generously with olive oil, cover lightly, and let rise in a warm place until puffy; it takes about 30 minutes.

Slash an "X" across the top of the loaf with a very sharp knife or razor blade. Beat the remaining egg yolk with the cold water and brush over loaf. Bake in a 350° oven for about 35 minutes or until well browned. Cool slightly on a wire rack before cutting. (To reheat cold loaf, wrap in foil and place in a 350° oven for 25 minutes.) Makes 1 loaf.

Panettone

A moderately sweet, cake-like bread, panettone is one of the specialties of Milan. Leavened either with yeast or with baking powder (as this one is), it is baked in many shapes, but most traditionally it is formed within a high round metal mold or collar of paper.

Inventive Italian-American cooks found that a small paper bag was easier to use than the tied paper collar (the molds were not readily available in this country), and the resulting shape has a curious and charming mushroom outline.

Serve with a sweet wine or espresso.

1 egg
2 egg yolks
¾ cup sugar
½ cup (¼ lb.) melted butter or margarine, cooled to lukewarm
1 teaspoon grated lemon peel
1 teaspoon each anise seed and anise extract
¼ cup each pine nuts (pignoli), dark raisins, and coarsely chopped, mixed candied fruit
3 cups all-purpose flour
2 teaspoons baking powder
½ teaspoon salt
1 cup milk

Beat egg, egg yolks, and sugar together until thick and pale yellow. Beat in the melted butter, then add lemon peel, anise seed, anise extract, pine nuts, raisins, and candied fruit. Sift and measure flour; sift flour again with baking powder and salt. Blend half the flour mixture with batter. Stir in half the milk, add remaining flour, and mix well. Add remaining milk and blend thoroughly.

Fold down top of a paper bag (a No. 6 or one that measures 3½ by 6 inches on the bottom) to form a cuff that is about 2¾ inches high. Butter bag generously, set on a baking sheet, and pour in batter.

Bake in a 325° oven for about 1 hour and 45 minutes or until bread is well browned and tests done when wooden skewer is inserted.

To serve hot, tear off paper bag and cut bread in wedges. To serve cold, wrap bread (still in bag) in a clean cloth, then in foil and let cool completely to mellow flavors. To reheat, wrap bread in foil and place in a 350° oven for 45 minutes. Makes 1 loaf.

To bake in a panettone pan, grease and flour dust a 6-inch wide, 4-inch deep panettone mold and bake as directed above.

Colomba di Pasqua

One of the most beautiful breads of Italy is the Easter dove. It is exceptionally delicious, not difficult to make or shape, and perfect for an Easter brunch. Serve slices plain or buttered.

1 package yeast, active dry or compressed
¼ cup warm water (lukewarm for compressed yeast)
½ cup milk
½ cup (¼ lb.) soft butter
10 tablespoons (½ cup plus 2 tablespoons) sugar
2 tablespoons grated lemon peel
2 teaspoons vanilla
½ teaspoon salt
3 eggs
3 egg yolks
   About 4½ cups unsifted all-purpose flour
   About 4 ounces (4 to 5 tablespoons or half an 8-oz. can) almond paste, cut in ½-inch cubes
   About 36 whole blanched almonds
   Beaten egg white and granulated sugar for decoration

Stir yeast into warm water and set aside to soften. Heat milk to scalding; cool.

In the large bowl of your mixer, cream butter, sugar, lemon peel, vanilla, and salt until mixture is fluffy. Beat in eggs and egg yolks, one at a time. Mix in milk and yeast; then at slow speed gradually beat in the 4½ cups flour. Turn soft dough onto well floured board; knead vigorously until smooth and quite elastic; takes 10 to 15 minutes.

Put dough in a large buttered bowl; turn over once to grease top. Cover bowl and set in a warm place for about 1 hour and 30 minutes, or until dough is doubled in volume.

To shape the dove, knead dough on lightly floured board to remove bubbles. Cut in half and shape each half into a smooth ball.

In the center of a greased 12 by 15-inch baking sheet, flatten one dough ball and roll out across narrow dimension of pan to make an oval about 11 inches long and 6 inches wide. On a floured board, roll the other ball of dough out to make a softly outlined triangle about 14 inches tall and 6 inches across wide end. Lay triangle across oval. Twist narrow end to make head; pinch tip to form beak. Twist wide end to make tail (see right); pull tail into fan shape and cut gashes to simulate feathers.

Stick almond paste chunks into wings and stud with almonds. Let rise in a warm place about 25 minutes, or until slightly puffed looking. Brush gently with beaten egg white and sprinkle wings gen-

Push almond paste into wings formed by dough oval. The body is a triangle twisted to define head and tail.

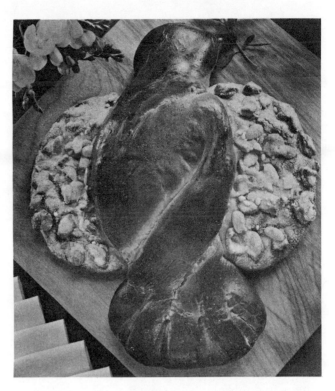

Dove of Easter is a charming Italian bread for this holiday. It's delightful served warm for breakfast or during the day.

erously with sugar. Bake in a 325° oven for about 50 minutes, until bird is richly browned; for lighter color you can cover bird with foil the last 15 minutes.

Serve warm or cool, cut wings from body and offer slices of both sections. (To make ahead, cool bread completely on a wire rack, then wrap airtight and freeze. Thaw before reheating.) To reheat bread, wrap in foil, and place in a 250° oven for 40 minutes. Makes 1 large loaf.

Buccellati

Ring shaped buccellati are from Lucca but can be found throughout Tuscany. In the fall they are made with fresh grapes instead of raisins. You start with the Colomba di Pasqua dough, making the appropriate flavor variations.

Prepare dough for the preceding Colomba di Pasqua with these changes: Combine ⅓ cup seeded muscat raisins with 3 tablespoons Marsala or Port wine; set aside for at least 30 minutes. Add 2 tablespoons anise seed to milk before scalding. Omit lemon peel and vanilla and use in their place 1 teaspoon anise extract. When you add liquid ingredients to the egg mixture, also add the wine drained from the raisins.

After you knead the dough, flatten with your hands until ¾ inch thick. Spread drained raisins over surface and roll jelly-roll-fashion, enclosing raisins and tucking ends under; let rise in a buttered bowl, covered until double in bulk.

To shape buccellati, knead out air bubbles and divide dough into thirds; knead each third into a smooth ball. On a greased baking sheet roll each portion of dough into a round cake 7 inches in diameter. Poke a hole in the exact center of each cake.

Shape into smooth rings by pulling from the center out with your hands in evenly pressured opposition. Make the center opening 6 inches across. Omit almonds, almond paste, and egg white and sugar decoration. Let rings rise in a warm place for about 25 minutes, or until puffed looking. Brush with 1 beaten whole egg. Bake in a 350° oven for 30 minutes, or until well browned.

Serve warm or cool; if bread is frozen for storage, thaw, wrap in foil, and reheat in a 250° oven for 30 minutes. Serve with butter. Makes 3 rings.

Pandoro di Verona

A Christmas specialty from Verona, this golden yeast loaf is moistened almost entirely by eggs, layered with butter, and shaped in such a way as to create its characteristic "vertical" texture. This means that if the bread is pulled apart, the pieces strip off in fragile fibers from top to bottom.

1 package yeast, active dry or compressed
¼ cup warm water (lukewarm for compressed
   yeast)
3 tablespoons sugar
¼ teaspoon salt
1 tablespoon melted butter or margarine
3 whole eggs
3 egg yolks
2 teaspoons vanilla
1 teaspoon grated lemon peel
   About 2½ cups unsifted all-purpose flour
½ cup (¼ lb.) soft butter or margarine
   Powdered sugar
   Butter (optional)

Mix yeast with water and let stand a few minutes until softened. In a large bowl beat together with a spoon the sugar, salt, melted butter, eggs, egg yolks, vanilla, and lemon peel. Mix in the yeast, then add 1 cup of the flour, beating until smoothly blended. Beat in another 1 cup flour until smoothly blended, then work in thoroughly another ½ cup flour (use 2½ cups flour total). Scrape dough down into the bowl, cover, set in a warm place and let rise until more than doubled in volume; takes about 2½ hours.

Vigorously beat dough with spoon to remove all air bubbles. Pour soft dough onto a well floured pastry cloth, turning to coat sticky surfaces. Gingerly knead dough for 5 minutes or until quite velvety and springy; the dough is unusually soft but easy to handle if you take care not to puncture the surface with your fingers.

Wrap dough in flour-dusted clear plastic film and chill about 20 minutes to make dough easier to roll.

Cover rolling pin with a stockinet cover for easier handling, and roll out dough on the floured pastry cloth to make an 11 or 12-inch square. Gently spread the ½ cup soft butter evenly to within about 1 inch of the edges. Fold in overlapping thirds, then roll out again to a 12-inch square.

Fold in overlapping thirds again, this time folding the dough at right angles to the preceding fold. (Protect dough with ample flour as you work; dust off excess before enclosing folds.) Roll to a 12-inch square; repeat this fold-and-roll procedure two more times, crossing each fold at right angles to the preceding one. Cover with clear plastic film and chill about 20 minutes to firm dough slightly, then fold and roll four more times.

Fold the 12-inch square in half, then roll up snugly from a narrow end and fit dough, folded edge up, into a heavily buttered and floured 3 to 4-quart tall mold (plain or fancy).

Cover and let rise until dough fills mold about two-thirds full; this usually takes at least 1 hour in a warm place.

Place on a low rack in a 350° oven and bake for 40 to 45 minutes or until bread is richly browned and a wooden skewer inserted into center comes out clean. Invert mold over a wire rack, tapping to release bread; leave bread upright, bracing, if needed. When the bread is cool enough to serve, if necessary, trim a bit off the base to make it sit steady.

Serve the bread while still warm or let it cool. Wrap airtight and store at room temperature for up to two days, or freeze for longer storage. To reheat, wrap thawed bread in foil and place in a 350° oven for about 20 minutes.

To serve, place pandoro on a platter and dust with powdered sugar. Slice bread thinly from the top, cutting at a 45° angle and taking every other slice from the opposite side of the loaf. Serve plain or spread with butter. Makes 12 to 16 servings.

Fit rolled spiral of dough vertically into buttered, floured mold; the end of the loaf may unfurl somewhat as bread bakes.

Drifts of powdered sugar accentuate shape of pandoro, a classic Italian Christmas bread: use any tall mold to give form.

Desserts
The Grand Finale

Fruit, zabaglione, fancy pastries, cookies

The climax of a meal in Italy is so diverse, ranging from utter simplicity to artistic grandeur, that one's taste cannot help but be satisfied.

Fruits of the season, fresh or cooked, take first priority. A bit of robustly flavored or rich cheese (see page 81) is another agreeable menu conclusion, and it may be served with or follow the fruit.

Then come desserts of classic fame. Here we explore them through hot foamy zabaglione, chilly zuppa inglese, frozen spumoni, crisp meringues, lavish tortes or tortas, and some interesting cookies. Generally, the more complicated preparations are broken down in easily manageable steps that can be completed in advance.

Red Wine Poached Bartlett Pears

In the autumn, platters of poached pears standing in their own sweet cooking liquid are a common sight on the sideboards of Roman restaurants.

- 6 firm-ripe medium to large Bartlett pears
- 1¾ cups dry red wine (or a 2/5-qt. bottle)
- 1 cup sugar
- ¼ teaspoon anise seed
- 2 sticks whole cinnamon, each 3 or 4 inches long
- 2 or 3 thin unpeeled lemon slices

In a saucepan large enough to hold the 6 pears side by side, combine the wine, sugar, anise, cinnamon, and lemon. Bring to a boil, stirring until sugar is dissolved. Remove core from blossom ends of the pears, leaving stem in place. Peel fruit or not, as

desired. Set fruit into boiling syrup and boil, covered, about 8 to 10 minutes, turning fruit occasionally so all portions are at times in the syrup. When fruit is heated through and still holds its shape, lift from syrup with a slotted spoon and transfer to a serving dish.

Boil syrup at high heat, uncovered, until reduced to ¾ to 1 cup. Pour hot syrup over and around pears. Serve warm or at room temperature. Serves 6.

Chestnuts Muddled in Port

More an after dinner snack than a dessert, chestnuts are roasted until moist and steamy, then saturated with a mixture of sugar and Port. Accompany with Port for sipping.

- 1 pound fresh chestnuts
- ½ cup Ruby or Tinta Port
- ¼ cup sugar
   Moistened cloth napkins

With a sharp pointed knife cut a slit about ½ inch long through shell into meat of each chestnut (this keeps them from exploding in the oven); discard any with mold. Arrange nuts in a single layer on a baking sheet; bake at 400° for 40 minutes. Also, mix Port and sugar in a deep bowl.

Remove chestnuts from oven. Using a thick potholder to protect your hand, squeeze each nut to pop the shell open so it can absorb the Port; drop nuts into Port-sugar mixture, stirring with each addition. Let stand until cool enough to touch comfortably, stirring occasionally. Transfer nuts to a serving bowl.

To eat, peel nuts with your hands, using the moist napkins for clean-up. Makes 6 to 8 servings.

Plums in Port

Port blends perfectly with the winey overtones of these late season plums; their flavor is best if they're allowed to stand a day or two before serving.

>   Unpeeled center slice of an orange, cut ½
>   inch thick
> 6   whole cloves
> 4   cups whole purple prune plums, each
>   slashed on one side to the pit
> 1   cup Tinta or Ruby Port
> ½   cup sugar
> 1   stick whole cinnamon, 3 or 4 inches long

Cut orange in quarters and stud with cloves. Combine in a saucepan with plums, Port, sugar, and cinnamon. Bring to a boil and simmer, uncovered, about 10 minutes or until fruit just begins to soften; time varies with size and ripeness of fruit. Cool, remove cinnamon, then chill. The sauce and fruit develop richer flavor after a day or two in the refrigerator; serve with juices. Makes 6 to 8 servings.

Basic Zabaglione

One of the best one-act food shows is the dramatic, at-the-table preparation of zabaglione. You can cook it over a denatured alcohol flame in the half-sphere shaped zabaglione pan, whipping egg yolks, wine, and a little sugar to a gold, velvety foam in about 5 minutes. Then pour it into fragile glasses to eat with a spoon, accompanied by crisp almond macaroons or dainty ladyfinger cookies.

You can also cook zabaglione in the kitchen in a double boiler.

Any number of fine variations of zabaglione are served hot or cold. This basic recipe gets you started.

> 8   egg yolks
> 3   to 4 tablespoons sugar
> ½   cup dry Sauterne, dry Semillon, Malvasia
>   Bianca, Marsala, Madeira, or sweet
>   Muscatel

In a round bottom zabaglione pan or top of a double boiler, beat together egg yolks, 3 tablespoons of the sugar, and the wine. Place the round bottom pan over direct heat (gas, electric, or denatured alcohol flame), or set the double boiler over gently simmering water. Whip mixture constantly with a wire whip until it is thick enough to briefly retain a slight peak when whip is withdrawn; it takes about 5 minutes, more or less.

Taste, and add the remaining sugar if desired. Pour into stemmed glasses (it is not hot enough to require preheating glasses) and serve at once. Makes 6 to 8 servings.

Zabaglione with Grenadine:

Add ½ teaspoon vanilla to Basic Zabaglione made with dry Sauterne, dry Semillon, or Malvasia Bianca. Pour ½ inch chilled grenadine in the bottom of each serving glass, fill; dust each serving with nutmeg.

Anisette Zabaglione:

Add 2 teaspoons anisette and ¼ teaspoon grated lemon peel to Basic Zabaglione made with dry Sauterne or dry Semillon.

Sherry Zabaglione:

Add 1 tablespoon dry Sherry to Basic Zabaglione made with dry Sauterne or dry Semillon.

Zabaglione with Cream:

Spoon a little sweetened, ice-cold whipped cream into the bottom of each serving glass and top with any hot zabaglione.

Marsala Zabaglione:

Make Basic Zabaglione increasing egg yolks to 12 and Marsala to 1½ cups.

Cognac Zabaglione:

Make Basic Zabaglione using 6 egg yolks, 6 tablespoons sugar, and ¼ cup cognac instead of wine. Makes 4 to 6 servings.

Rum Zabaglione:

Make Basic Zabaglione using 8 egg yolks, ¼ cup sugar, ⅓ cup dry white wine, and 3 tablespoons light rum. Let cool to room temperature or cover and chill.

Place 8 scoops vanilla ice cream in 8 individual bowls. Top equally with a mixture of ½ cup blueberries (fresh or frozen, thawed) and 2 cups hulled strawberries, then spoon on the zabaglione and sprinkle with semisweet chocolate curls (pare ½ oz. chocolate with a vegetable peeler). Makes 8 servings.

Chilled Zabaglione Cream

Gelatin stabilizes this smooth, rich, zabaglione-based dessert.

6   tablespoons sugar
1   teaspoon unflavored gelatin
½   cup Marsala or dry Sherry
6   egg yolks
1   tablespoon brandy or ¼ teaspoon brandy
      flavoring
1   teaspoon vanilla
1   cup whipping cream
3   egg whites
⅛   teaspoon each salt and cream of tartar
½   ounce semisweet chocolate, cut in curls or
      grated

In the top of a double boiler, mix together 4 tablespoons of the sugar and gelatin. Stir in wine. Beat egg yolks until thick and lighter in color and stir into gelatin mixture. Cook over hot water, stirring constantly, until thickened. Remove from heat and stir in brandy and vanilla. Chill until cool but not set; stir occasionally.

Whip cream until stiff and fold into egg yolk mixture. Beat egg whites until foamy, add salt and cream of tartar, and beat until stiff. Beat in the re-maining 2 tablespoons sugar. Fold meringue into the egg yolk mixture and spoon into 6 to 8 tall, slender parfait glasses or dessert dishes. Chill for 1 hour or longer. Garnish with chocolate curls. Makes 6 to 8 servings.

Panforte di Siena

A unique confection that is a cross between fruit-cake and candy, panforte (or strong bread) from Siena is solid with whole almonds and just enough candied and fresh fruit peels, flour, spices, and a honey-sugar syrup to bind the nuts together. Serve in small wedges with espresso, tea, brandy, or dessert wines.

¾   pound (2 cups) whole, unblanched
      almonds
1   cup candied orange peel, coarsely chopped
1   cup candied lemon peel, put through fine
      blade of a food chopper
1   teaspoon grated lemon peel
1   teaspoon ground cinnamon
½   teaspoon ground coriander
¼   teaspoon each ground cloves and ground
      nutmeg
½   cup unsifted all-purpose flour
¾   cup each sugar and honey
2   tablespoons butter or margarine
      Powdered sugar

Mix almonds with candied orange peel, candied lemon peel, grated lemon peel, cinnamon, coriander, cloves, nutmeg, and flour until flour coats each particle. Combine sugar, honey, and butter in a deep pan and bring quickly to 265° (hard ball stage), stirring frequently. Pour the hot syrup into the almond mixture, blending thoroughly.

Have ready an 8 or 9-inch cake pan with removable bottom, buttered heavily, the bottom lined with brown paper, buttered heavily again, and dusted with flour. Pour batter into cake pan and spread evenly.

Bake in a 300° oven for 45 minutes, then cool thoroughly. Panforte should be firm to touch. Release sides of cake from pan with a knife, then invert onto a large sheet of waxed paper or clear plastic wrap heavily dusted with powdered sugar.

Remove brown paper from bottom of cake, cutting away if necessary. Heavily dust top of panforte with more powdered sugar to coat completely, then place in a plastic bag or more clear plastic wrap to keep airtight. Panforte can be served immediately or stored airtight indefinitely. Serve in small wedges. Makes about 2½ pounds confection.

Cheeses-a Savory Climax and a Good Beginning

An Italian will laughingly describe the cheeses chosen to end a meal as cheese to make you strong. The little joke comes from the fact that Italians like cheeses with character for dessert.

A selection of those they like that you can also find in this country might include several of the following: one or more firm Parmesans at different stages of aging; mellow-sharp Asiago; sharp pecorino; rich and pungent, veined gorgonzola; tangy provolone; as well as the smooth but flavorfully well-defined Bel Paese.

Quite often, the cheeses make a course in themselves, accompanied by a heavily crusted piece of bread and a glass of wine. But when complementary fruits like juicy pears, plump grapes, or golden-fleshed peaches are in season, then the cheese and fruit would likely be savored together.

At breakfast, the addition of cheese is a favored way to give more staying quality to this light meal that typically consists of just coffee and milk with some sort of bread. Occasionally a chunk of cheese may accompany the bread, or the bread is spread with ricotta and sprinkled with salt and pepper or drizzled with honey.

Sift powdered sugar onto the warm cake to make a topping.

Florentine Corn Meal Cake

Corn meal lends a pleasing crunch and nutlike flavor to this pound cake also known as amor polenta.

Traditionally it is baked in a special pan (with a rounded, ridged bottom) called either a deerback, saddle mold, or nutbread loaf pan. It can also be cooked in standard baking pans.

- ⅔ cup soft butter
- 2⅔ cups sifted powdered sugar
- 1 teaspoon vanilla
- 2 whole eggs
- 1 egg yolk
- 1¼ cups cake flour
- ⅓ cup yellow corn meal
  About 2 tablespoons powdered sugar

In a large bowl of an electric mixer, beat butter with the 2⅔ cups sugar until creamy. Beat in vanilla; then add eggs and yolk, one at a time, beating well after each addition. Sift and measure flour, then mix with corn meal. Add flour mixture, a portion at a time, to batter, blending well after each addition.

Generously grease and flour dust either a 10-inch deerback pan, an 8½ by 4½-inch loaf pan, or a 3½ to 4 cup tube mold pan. Spoon batter into pan and spread evenly.

Bake in a 325° oven for about 1 hour and 15 minutes or until a wooden pick, inserted in center, comes out clean, and the cake springs back when lightly touched in the center.

Cool cake in pan for 3 minutes, then turn it out onto a wire rack. Sift the 2 tablespoons sugar over the warm cake. Let cool completely, then slice thinly. Makes about 15 servings.

Torta

Swiss chard is the base of this unusual northern Italian dessert pie. Some cooks add chocolate, but we prefer this simpler combination that in many ways resembles a steamed fruit pudding. The amount of sugar varies according to taste; start with the small amount, adding more if you like.

Pastry:

- 6 cups all-purpose flour
- 1 teaspoon baking powder
- 1 teaspoon salt
- ½ cup sugar
- ½ cup (¼ lb.) butter or margarine
- 2 cups shortening
- ½ cup water
- ¼ cup whiskey (or ¼ cup water and 1 teaspoon vanilla)

Filling:

- 1¼ cups cooked, drained, and ground Swiss chard
- ⅓ cup cooked, drained, and ground Italian (or regular curly) parsley
- 6½ cups stale French bread pieces (soaked in water and squeezed dry before measuring, then crumbled)
- ⅓ cup each grated Parmesan cheese and grated dry jack cheese (or all Parmesan cheese)
- 2 cups dark seedless raisins
- ½ cup pine nuts (pignoli)
- 6 eggs, beaten
- 2 tablespoons whiskey (optional)
- ¼ to ½ cup sugar
- ½ teaspoon each salt and ground cinnamon
- ¼ teaspoon ground allspice

Topping:

- 1 egg, well beaten
- 1 teaspoon vanilla
- 1 tablespoon whiskey or water
- 1½ tablespoons sugar
  Butter or margarine

Sift and measure flour for pastry; sift again with baking powder, salt, and sugar into a large bowl. Work in butter and shortening with your hands until crumbly. Stir in water and whiskey with a fork to form a dough. Cover and chill.

For the filling, combine chard, parsley, bread, cheeses, raisins, pine nuts, eggs, whiskey, sugar, salt, cinnamon, and allspice; beat until well mixed.

Divide pastry in 4 equal portions. Roll out each portion on a lightly floured board to form a fairly even circle about 3/16 inch thick. Fit each crust into a buttered 9-inch pie pan; leave 2 to 3 inches of dough overhanging edges all around. Divide filling equally among the pastry shells.

Form the edges of the crust in this manner to make becco (or beak) rim: roll overhanging dough on one side of the pan up to the inside edge of the rim. Cut with a knife down through the dough roll to the rim of the pan. Fold the cut edge on your left diagonally over the rim so it is parallel with the inside edge, pressing to the rim to seal. Make another cut to the rim about 1 inch to the left of the first cut. Turn this cut edge over as before. Working around to your left, continue the roll, repeating the cutting and turning until all rim is complete.

For topping, blend egg, vanilla, whiskey, and sugar, and spread about 2 tablespoons of this mixture over each pie; dot each section of crust rim with butter. Bake in a 350° oven for glass pie plates, or a 375° oven for metal pans, for 55 minutes or until crust is deep golden brown. Serve warm or cool, cut in wedges. (To freeze, cool completely, then wrap airtight; unwrap to thaw.) Makes 4 tortas; each makes 6 to 8 servings.

Pine Nut Torte

Canned almond paste and pine nuts are the base of this moist cake that bakes in a crust.

Crust:
- 2 tablespoons sugar
- 1 cup unsifted all-purpose flour
- 6 tablespoons butter or margarine
- 1 egg
- ¼ cup raspberry jam

Filling:
- 1 can (8 oz.) almond paste
- 6 eggs, separated
- ¼ cup each sugar and all-purpose flour
- ¾ teaspoon baking powder
- ¾ cup toasted pine nuts (directions follow)
  Sugar

Mix sugar and flour for crust in a small bowl. Add butter and rub with your fingers until mixture is fine crumbs. Stir in egg well with a fork, then press dough into a ball. Roll out to 12 to 13-inch diameter circle and fit into a 10-inch-diameter cake pan (or cheese cake pan) with removable bottom. Press dough smoothly into pan, making a 1-inch-high rim. Spread jam over dough.

Combine almond paste for filling in a bowl with egg yolks, sugar, flour, and baking powder and beat (preferably with an electric mixer) until smoothly

blended. Whip egg whites until they hold short distinct peaks. Beat about half the egg whites into the almond batter, then fold in remaining whites and a generous ½ cup of the pine nuts.

Pour batter into prepared crust. Scatter the remaining pine nuts over surface. Bake in a 350° oven for 35 minutes or until center feels firm when lightly touched. Cool slightly (or completely); remove pan rim and sprinkle with sugar before cutting. Makes 10 to 12 portions.

To toast pine nuts (pignoli), spread shelled nuts in a single layer in a pan; bake in a 350° oven for about 5 minutes or until pale gold, shaking occasionally.

Neapolitan Cake

Chocolate, raspberries, brandy, and a cooked butter cream flavor this refrigerator cake.

- 4 egg yolks
- ¾ cup sugar
- ¼ cup water
- ⅔ cup soft butter or margarine
- 2 tablespoons brandy or cognac
- 2 chiffon cake layers (each 9-inch diameter; made from a cake mix or from a bakery)
- 1 cup raspberry jelly
  Chocolate frosting (recipe follows)

Using an electric mixer beat egg yolks until thick and light colored. Meanwhile combine sugar and water in a small saucepan, bring to a boil, and insert a candy thermometer. Boil uncovered, without stirring, until temperature reaches 238°. Pour hot syrup in a slow stream into the egg yolks while beating constantly; when syrup is added continue to beat until the thick mixture has cooled to room temperature. Beat in soft butter and brandy.

Split each cake layer in half horizontally and place 1 layer on a cake plate. Heat jelly until melted and spread half of it over cake on the plate. Top with a second cake layer and spread it with half of the butter cream. Set on third cake layer and spread it with remaining jelly. Top with final cake layer. Spread cake sides with remaining butter cream. Spread top of cake with chocolate frosting; chill. Makes 10 to 12 servings.

Chocolate frosting: Melt 2 ounces unsweetened chocolate in a small bowl over hot water. Mix in 2 tablespoons soft butter or margarine. Mix in 1 cup unsifted powdered sugar alternately with 3 tablespoons milk. If needed, add more milk to make a frosting that spreads easily. Stir in 1 teaspoon vanilla.

Zuppa Inglese

Mixes provide a shortcut in the making of this rum custard cake. Zuppa Inglese has many variations; among the most popular are those flavored with fruit or chocolate. If made a day ahead, zuppa Inglese cuts and serves best.

> **Orange cake (directions follow)**
> **Orange-rum syrup (directions follow)**
> **Rum custard (directions follow)**
> ½ **cup whipping cream**
> **Sugar**
> **Slivered toasted almonds (optional)**

Remove pan side from cake, leaving cake on base. Carefully cut cake horizontally into three equal layers and lift off the top two layers. Replace pan sides around pan bottom holding the remaining cake layer.

Drizzle cake bottom layer with ⅓ of the orange-rum syrup, then cover with ⅓ of the rum custard. Carefully place the middle layer of cake on the custard, sprinkle this layer with another ⅓ of the syrup, and top with another ⅓ of the custard. Set the top cake layer in place, sprinkle with the remaining syrup, pour on the remaining custard, spreading evenly. (If cake is baked in a 9-inch pan, you may have custard left over.)

Chill cake for at least 6 hours or overnight; cover lightly so the top will not be marred. Remove pan sides. Whip the cream until stiff, sweeten slightly with sugar, and spread on cake sides. Garnish top of cake with nuts, if desired. Cut in wedges. Makes 10 to 12 servings.

Orange cake: Prepare 1 package (about 1 lb. 2 oz.) yellow cake mix according to directions on the package, adding to the batter ¾ teaspoon grated orange peel. Grease and flour dust a 9 or 10-inch cheesecake

pan (at least 2¾ inches deep) with removable bottom or sides. Pour in the cake batter and bake in a 350° oven for 40 to 45 minutes or until a wooden skewer inserted into center comes out clean. Let cake cool completely in pan on a wire rack.

Orange-rum syrup: Combine in a small saucepan 6 tablespoons water, 6 tablespoons sugar, 1 teaspoon grated orange peel, and ½ teaspoon grated lemon peel. Bring to boiling and simmer rapidly for 3 minutes. Remove from heat and let cool; blend in 5 tablespoons light rum.

Rum custard: Blend 1 large box (4½ oz.) no-bake custard mix with 2½ cups milk. Bring to a boil, stirring. Remove from heat and set in cold water to cool quickly, stirring frequently to keep mixture soft. Beat 1 cup whipping cream until stiff. Fold into cooled custard, along with 4 tablespoons light rum. Use at once.

Chocolate Rum Custard Cake:

Follow the directions for Zuppa Inglese, making these changes: use 1 package (about 1 lb. 2 oz.) chocolate cake mix instead of the yellow cake mix; prepare as directed on the package, then bake, cool, and split as directed for Orange cake.

Make the Orange-rum syrup, omitting the lemon peel. Make the Rum custard exactly the same, or add, if you like, ¼ cup ground sweet chocolate for a mild chocolate flavor.

Then fill, chill, frost, and garnish the cake as directed.

Chiffon Gateau St. Honoré

The French claim gateau St. Honoré as their own, but the Italians take many creative liberties with this cream puff cake.

This one has an airy chiffon filling and is flavored with chocolate. Make the cream puffs and the pastry base first.

> 1 **envelope unflavored gelatin**
> ¼ **cup cold water**
> 4 **eggs, separated**
> ½ **cup sugar**
> ¼ **cup rum or ½ teaspoon rum flavoring**
> 1 **teaspoon vanilla**
> 1 **cup whipping cream**
> 1½ **tablespoons each cocoa and water**
> **About 14 cream puffs (directions follow)**
> **Press-in pastry crust (directions follow)**

Soften gelatin in the ¼ cup water for 5 minutes; heat to dissolve completely. Set in a bowl of lukewarm water to keep liquid. With an electric mixer, beat egg whites at high speed until foamy, then gradually beat in ½ cup of the sugar; beat until whites form shiny peaks that just bend over when beaters are lifted out.

Without washing the beaters, beat egg yolks with remaining ¼ cup sugar until thick; beat in the gelatin, rum, and vanilla. Whip cream until stiff, then fold cream, egg whites, and yolk mixture together until blended.

In a small bowl, stir together the cocoa and 1½ tablespoons water to blend, then measure out 1½ cups of the whipped chiffon mixture and blend well with the chocolate.

To determine how many of the cream puffs you will need, set them in the pan with press-in pastry, fitting closely together against the pan rim to make a ring.

Then remove cream puffs from pan and spoon into each about 1 tablespoon of the light color chiffon mixture or enough to fill. Spoon the remaining light color chiffon mixture onto the crust, spreading evenly. Set filled puffs on filling in a ring against pan rim. Spoon chocolate chiffon mixture into the center of the ring. Cover and chill until firm; takes about 3 hours. Though you can make the dessert early in the day, it is best served within 12 hours. Cut in wedges allowing 1 cream puff for each portion. Makes about 14 servings.

Cream puffs: In a 2-quart saucepan, combine ½ cup water, 4 tablespoons butter, ⅛ teaspoon salt, and 1 tablespoon sugar. Heat mixture until butter melts. Meanwhile, measure 1 cup unsifted all-purpose flour and set aside.

Bring butter mixture to a rapid boil. Add flour all at once and remove pan from heat. With a wooden spoon, beat mixture vigorously until it is a smooth paste that pulls away from pan sides. Beat in 2 eggs, one at a time, until thoroughly blended and paste is smooth and glossy. Let stand for 15 minutes.

For each puff, spoon 1 tablespoon of the paste on a lightly greased baking sheet; leave 1½ inches between each puff. Bake in a 375° oven for about 30 minutes, or until firm and dry to touch. Cut a 2-inch slit around the base of each puff. Cool on a wire rack. Makes about 16 cream puffs.

Press-in pastry crust: In a bowl combine 1 cup unsifted all-purpose flour, 2 tablespoons sugar, and 6 tablespoons butter. With your fingers, rub mixture together until it is of even texture. With your hands compress mixture into a smooth ball that doesn't crumble.

Place the dough in a 9 or 10-inch cheesecake pan with removable bottom or sides and press it out in a firm, even layer. Bake in a 325° oven for 30 minutes or until light golden brown; cool.

Ice Cream Gateau St. Honoré

Once the cream puffs are baked, this is an impressive, quickly made dessert.

1 cup finely crushed vanilla wafer crumbs
2 tablespoons melted butter or margarine
  About 14 cream puffs (see Chiffon Gateau
   St. Honoré, preceding recipe)
2 quarts chocolate ice cream, slightly
   softened
2 tablespoons each powdered sugar and rum
   (or ½ teaspoon rum flavoring)
1 cup whipping cream
1 ounce semisweet chocolate, cut in curls
   with a vegetable peeler

In a 9 or 10-inch cheesecake pan with removable bottom or sides, blend wafer crumbs well with butter. Pat mixture out evenly over the bottom of the pan. Bake in a 325° oven for 5 minutes; cool.

To determine the number of cream puffs you will need, place them close together on crumb crust in a ring around pan edge; remove puffs from pan.

Working quickly, fill each puff with ice cream. Pack the remaining ice cream in an even layer on crumb crust and set puffs around the edge. Set in the freezer while you whip the cream until stiff; flavor cream with the sugar and rum. Mound cream in the center of cream puff ring. Cover and freeze until firm; takes about 5 hours at about 0°. You can wrap this dessert airtight and store up to 2 weeks in the freezer. To serve, remove pan sides and let stand about 10 minutes at room temperature. Sprinkle with chocolate curls and cut between each puff to make a portion. Makes about 14 servings.

Cassata

Contrasting colors of ice cream are layered in a mold; the center is fruit-flavored whipped cream.

- 1½ quarts vanilla ice cream, softened slightly
- 1 quart chocolate ice cream, softened slightly
- 1 cup whipping cream
- 1 teaspoon vanilla or 1 tablespoon Maraschino liqueur
- 1 egg white
- 2 tablespoons each powdered sugar, chopped candied red cherries, chopped candied citron, and chopped candied orange peel

  Whole candied red cherries and pieces of candied citron

Line a 2-quart mold evenly with the vanilla ice cream. Freeze until very firm at about 0°. Cover the vanilla ice cream with an even layer of the chocolate ice cream; freeze until very firm. Whip ½ cup of the cream until stiff and blend in the vanilla. Whip the egg white until soft peaks form then beat in the sugar until stiff. Fold egg white into cream along with the chopped cherries, citron, and orange peel. Spoon this mixture into the center of the molded ice cream; spread to make a smooth bottom layer. Cover and freeze until firm (store as long as 2 weeks in the freezer).

To unmold, dip the mold to the rim in hot water for about 6 seconds, then invert onto a cold serving plate. If the ice cream does not come free immediately, dip in water again for 2 or 3 seconds. Return to freezer for at least 30 minutes to refirm surface before serving (or you can wrap unmolded cassata and store in the freezer).

Whip the remaining cream until stiff and use to decorate the cassata, garnishing with whole cherries and pieces of citron. Allow to stand at room temperature for about 10 minutes, then cut in wedges. Makes 12 to 16 servings.

Tortoni Cups

Almond macaroons enhance this simple ice cream tortoni.

- 2 cups almond macaroon cooky crumbs, firmly packed
- 1 cup apricot jam or peach jam
- 1 quart slightly softened toasted almond ice cream
- 1 cup whipping cream

  Red and green candied cherries

Mix together the macaroon crumbs and the apricot or peach jam with a fork until the crumbs are coated with jam. Divide the crumb mixture evenly between paper-lined muffin cups—use 8 regular-size paper baking cups or 16 miniature paper baking cups—spread crumbs to cover bottoms of the cups. Top crumbs evenly with the slightly softened ice cream. Whip cream until stiff and swirl decoratively onto ice cream; top each tortoni with a candied cherry. Cover lightly with waxed paper. Freeze at about 0° until the tortoni is solid. Then wrap airtight and freeze until needed.

Remove from the freezer about 5 minutes before serving. Makes 8 to 16 servings.

Spumone

This lavishly rich tasting frozen mousse, flavored with anise liqueur, comes from Rome.

- 1 cup sugar
- ¾ cup water
- 6 egg yolks
- 2 cups whipping cream
- 2 teaspoons vanilla
- 3 tablespoons anisette or other anise-flavored liqueur
- ½ cup toasted, chopped blanched almonds (directions follow)

  Whole strawberries (optional)

Combine sugar and water in a saucepan and bring to a boil, stirring, until sugar is dissolved. Then continue to boil, uncovered, until syrup is 220° on a candy thermometer.

Meanwhile, in the top of a double boiler beat the yolks with an electric mixer until they are thick. Continue to beat the egg yolks and slowly pour the hot syrup into them; avoid pouring the syrup into the beaters. Place egg yolk mixture over slightly simmering water and continue to beat with mixer until stiff peaks form; takes about 7 minutes. Remove from heat and set double boiler in cold water; continue beating until mixture is cold. Whip cream until stiff and flavor with vanilla and anisette. Fold cream and nuts into the egg yolk mixture. Pour into a 1¾ to 2-quart mold; smooth the surface. Cover and freeze at about 0° until firm; store in freezer for as long as 2 weeks. Unmold and refirm surface as directed for Cassata (see left).

Serve decorated with strawberries; cut in thick vertical slices. Makes 8 to 10 servings.

Toasted almonds: Spread chopped, blanched almonds in a single layer in a rimmed baking pan. Place in a 350° oven for 5 to 10 minutes or until golden, stirring frequently. Let cool.

Chestnut Torte with Raspberries

The sweet, mellow flavor of chestnuts is widely popular in Italian desserts. To make this one, you can use cooked fresh chestnuts, whole chestnuts canned in water, or canned unsweetened chestnut purée.

    1½ cups cooked, peeled, unsweetened
          chestnuts
     5 eggs, separated
     ⅔ cup sugar
     ⅓ cup water
     ½ cup (¼ lb.) soft butter or margarine
     1 teaspoon vanilla
     2 tablespoons Cointreau or Curaçao
     ¾ cup sugar
     1 cup whipping cream
        Orange crust (recipe follows)
        Raspberry sauce (recipe follows)
        Mint leaves

Force cooked chestnuts through a food mill or a wire strainer; set purée aside. (If you use canned purée, measure 1½ cups.) Beat egg yolks until very thick and light in color. Meanwhile, boil the ⅔ cup sugar and water over high heat, uncovered, until mixture spins a thread (234°). Pour hot syrup slowly into yolks and beat constantly, carefully avoiding the beaters. Beat in purée, butter, vanilla, and liqueur.

With a clean beater, whip egg whites until stiff; then gradually add the ¾ cup sugar, beating constantly, until whites hold high, distinct, glossy peaks. Whip ½ cup of cream until stiff. Fold whites and cream into chestnut mixture and blend well. Pour mixture into orange crust-lined pan. Cover and freeze at about 0° until firm, at least 8 hours.

To release pan side, dip a towel in hot water and wring dry; wrap around pan and hold in place 30 seconds. Then remove towel and run a knife blade around edge of torte. Take away pan side. Set torte on serving dish. Whip remaining ½ cup cream until stiff and force through pastry bag with a fancy tip onto torte to decorate. Return torte to freezer, wrap airtight when cream is frozen, and store until ready to serve.

To serve, hold torte in refrigerator about 15 to 20 minutes before cutting. Garnish with a few raspberries from the sauce and a few mint leaves. Cut in wedges and spoon some of the sauce over each portion. Makes 12 to 16 servings.

Orange crust: Mix 1 cup finely crushed, orange-flavored wafer cooky crumbs with 2 tablespoons melted butter or margarine. Pat crumbs evenly over bottom of an 8 or 9-inch cheesecake pan (at least 2 inches deep) with removable bottom or sides.

Raspberry sauce: Sweeten 2 cups washed and hulled raspberries with sugar to taste. Add 3 to 5 tablespoons Cointreau or Curaçao, blend gently, cover, and chill about 1 hour before serving.

Strawberry Macaroon Torte

This ultra smooth torte softens rapidly, so serve it immediately.

     ½ pound small (about 1-inch diameter)
          almond macaroon cookies
     6 tablespoons dry Sherry
     6 egg yolks
     1 cup sugar
     ⅓ cup water
     1 cup whipping cream
     4 tablespoons kirsch (cherry brandy)
     ½ cup whipping cream
     2 tablespoons powdered sugar
     2 cups small whole or sliced strawberries

Combine the macaroons and Sherry in a small deep bowl and mix occasionally to thoroughly moisten cookies. Line the base of a 9-inch cheesecake pan with removable bottom or sides with the macaroons, filling in as completely as possible. Drizzle any remaining Sherry over the cookies and set pan aside.

Beat the egg yolks with an electric mixer at high speed until thick; meanwhile blend the sugar with water and boil rapidly, uncovered (stirring occasionally until clear), until syrup reaches 230° on a candy thermometer (spins a thread). Pour hot syrup gradually into the eggs as you beat them—avoid hitting beaters with syrup; continue to beat until mixture is very thick. Set pan in ice water until cool to touch; stir occasionally.

With the same beater, whip 1 cup of the cream until stiff and fold in 3 tablespoons of the kirsch and the egg yolk mixture. Pour into pan lined with macaroons. Cover and freeze at about 0° until firm, at least 8 hours.

Whip the remaining ½ cup cream and flavor with the 1 tablespoon kirsch and powdered sugar; spoon puffs of the cream decoratively around the edge of the torte; and return to freezer. Cover when firm.

Release torte from pan sides as directed in Chestnut Torte with Raspberries (preceding recipe). Spoon strawberries onto top and serve at once; cut into wedges. Makes about 10 servings.

Postprandial Torte

Regardless of how long this torte is frozen, its cloud-like texture is easy to cut. Liqueurs make up the flavor base; golden Galliano blends with chocolate flavored crème de cacao. Other combinations to consider: ½ cup light rum and ¼ teaspoon ground nutmeg in place of Galliano and crème de cacao; omit chocolate curls, dusting torte with nutmeg; or use green crème de menthe instead of the Galliano.

1 cup finely crushed chocolate-flavored
  wafer cooky crumbs or sugar cooky
  crumbs
3 tablespoons melted butter or margarine
4 eggs, separated
¼ cup sugar
1 cup whipping cream
¼ cup each Galliano liqueur and white crème
  de cacao
1 cup marshmallow cream
  About 4 ounces semisweet chocolate,
  shaved into curls with a vegetable peeler

Blend the cooky crumbs with melted butter and press in the bottom of a 9-inch cheesecake pan with removable bottom or sides; chill.

Beat the egg yolks and sugar with electric mixer at high speed until very thick. Using the same beater, whip the cream just until stiff. Then add the Galliano and crème de cacao, beating again until thick.

With clean beaters, beat the egg whites until stiff. Then add the marshmallow cream a dollop at a time, whipping constantly at high speed; continue beating until the whites hold sharp distinct peaks.

Fold thoroughly together the whites, cream, and egg yolks, and pour into the cooky crumb-lined pan. Cover and freeze at about 0° until firm, at least 8 hours. Pile on the chocolate curls, cover, and return to freezer until ready to serve. (You can store as long as 2 weeks in the freezer.) Release pan sides as directed in Chestnut Torte with Raspberries (page 87). Quickly place on a serving dish and cut into wedges. Makes 10 servings.

Italian Meringue

Unlike a regular meringue that is made just by beating egg whites and sugar, this combines whipped egg whites with a boiled sugar syrup. The result is an incredibly smooth, somewhat less rigid meringue foam that can be formed and baked as whimsical little round mushrooms to serve as you would a cooky. Or you can blend the uncooked meringue with butter, making a superbly delicate butter cream for pastries and frosting cakes.

Several critical points need to be considered in making this meringue. When the syrup reaches the proper temperature, begin at once to add it to the beating egg whites. You will need a sturdy electric mixer; a hand-held model won't do. Do not double the recipe, for the meringue does not beat up well in a wide bowl. And do not try to make this meringue on a rainy or highly humid day.

2 egg whites
1¼ cups sugar
½ cup water
⅛ teaspoon cream of tartar

Combine egg whites and ¼ cup sugar in the small bowl of an electric mixer and beat at highest speed until whites are very stiff and hold rigid peaks when the beater is withdrawn. (If whites get stiff before syrup is cooked, continue to beat at a very slow speed.)

While whites are beating, combine in a small saucepan the 1 cup sugar, water, and cream of tartar and cook over highest heat. Stir occasionally until sugar is dissolved; cook to 265° on a candy thermometer (soft crack stage). As spatters form on pan sides, wash them off with a wet pastry brush.

At once, pour hot syrup in a thin stream into the stiff egg whites, carefully avoiding the beaters, and beating at high speed. If syrup gets too thick to pour easily, reheat briefly; use all the syrup. (If you have a stationary bowl mixer, add syrup in about 6 portions, stopping for additions.) Continue beating for a minute or so after the syrup is incorporated; mixture should have a slightly thicker consistency than marshmallow cream. Use the meringue as directed below to make baked meringue mushrooms or butter cream.

Baked Italian Meringue Mushrooms:

Cool the Italian Meringue (one recipe's yield) at least 15 minutes at room temperature. Force the meringue through a pastry bag with a plain round metal tip (or no tip at all) onto a greased, flour-dusted baking sheet to make 10 or 12 mounded puffs about 2 inches in diameter. Shape remaining meringue in an equal number of puffs, each about 1-inch diameter at base.

Bake in a 200° oven for 1 hour. Turn off heat and leave in oven about 30 minutes more to dry; meringues should be very white. Cool on wire racks. (You can store in airtight containers for several weeks.)

To form mushrooms, lightly sift cocoa or ground sweet chocolate over the large meringue puffs, then set each puff on a smaller one. Use to decorate desserts such as a large mound of ice cream, or individual servings of ice cream, cakes, or molded desserts. Makes 10 to 12 mushrooms.

Italian Meringue Butter Cream:

Chill the Italian meringue (one recipe's yield) in the refrigerator for several hours or overnight. Beat until fluffy ½ cup (¼ lb.) sweet (unsalted) butter with flavoring of your choice: 1 tablespoon Cointreau, kirsch (cherry brandy), other liqueur, or 1 teaspoon vanilla. Then add the meringue in large spoonfuls, beating in thoroughly. Chill, covered, until ready to use. Makes about 2 cups, enough to frost a 2-layer, 9-inch cake (chill until ready to serve), or enough for the tea cakes below.

Italian Meringue Tea Cakes:

Cut frozen or freshly made pound cake in ¼-inch-thick slices. Spread thin layers of apricot jam between slices. Cut cakes in rounds or squares about 1½ inches across—makes 20 pieces. Drizzle each cake top with about ½ teaspoon Cointreau or kirsch. Force all the Italian Meringue Butter Cream through a pastry bag with plain round tip (or with no tip) to make small puffs on each cake. Cover without touching cream and chill until ready to serve. Makes 20 cakes.

Marengo Cavour

Essentially this make-ahead dessert is Florentine, but the coffee flavor in the chocolate and cream filling is an addition from the New World.

4 egg whites
½ teaspoon cream of tartar
1 cup sugar
1 teaspoon vanilla
   Cream filling (directions follow)
   Sweet ground chocolate or cocoa
   (optional)

In an electric mixer bowl that holds at least 6 cups below the top curve of the beater, combine the egg whites and cream of tartar. Beat at highest speed just until frothy (there should be no bottom layer of free-flowing viscous white). Continue beating and add the sugar, 1 tablespoon every minute, sprinkling it gradually over the mixing whites. When all the sugar is incorporated, add vanilla and beat 1 or 2 more minutes. When the beater is lifted out, the whites should hold very stiff, sharp, unbending peaks.

Grease and flour dust 2 baking sheets; trace an 8-inch circle on each. Using a pastry bag with a plain tip (or a spoon and spatula), pipe or spread about half the meringue onto one baking sheet. Shape remaining meringue in an 8-inch solid disk with a decorative surface of puffs and swirls.

Bake meringues in a 250° oven for 1½ hours (color should be pure white to faint amber). If you have two ovens, position each meringue just below the center in each oven. If you have one oven, position the meringues just above and below the center, then switch their positions halfway through baking.

Turn off heat and leave meringues in the closed oven for 3 to 4 hours to continue drying. Remove from oven. While pans are still warm, flex them to pop the meringue free but leave disks in place to cool. Store cooled disks airtight at room temperature as long as 5 days.

Place the plain meringue on a flat serving dish; spread all the cream filling evenly on just the top of the disk. Place the decorative meringue on the whipped cream. Cover and refrigerate for 8 hours or overnight to mellow for easy cutting. If desired, dust top lightly with sweet ground chocolate. Cut into wedges to serve. Makes 8 to 10 servings.

Cream filling: Blend 1 teaspoon instant coffee powder and 4 tablespoons coffee-flavored liqueur (or 2 additional teaspoons instant coffee powder, 2 tablespoons water, and 1 teaspoon vanilla). Beat 2 cups whipping cream until stiff, then fold in the liquid coffee mixture and 1 large bar (about 10 oz.) milk chocolate, coarsely chopped.

Seal oval of dough around aluminum tube; flare ends to facilitate filling the shells. Then fry in oil.

With cannoli, the traditional Sicilian ricotta-filled pastries, serve espresso coffee in tiny cups.

Cannoli

Crisp, cream-filled cannoli are a most tempting Sicilian pastry. They are based on thinly rolled dough wrapped around metal tubes, then fried to make crisp shells. You can use cannoli tubes (see page 6) or make your own: purchase 1-inch diameter lightweight aluminum tubing at a hardware store and have it cut into 4½-inch lengths.

Both the cannoli pastry shells and the ricotta filling can be made several days ahead, but should be put together just before serving so the shells will retain their crispness.

1¾ cups unsifted all-purpose flour
½ teaspoon salt
2 tablespoons sugar
1 egg, slightly beaten
2 tablespoons firm butter or margarine, cut in small pieces
    About ¼ cup dry Sauterne
1 egg white, slightly beaten
    Shortening or salad oil for deep frying
    Ricotta filling (choose one of the following)
    Powdered sugar
    Chopped milk chocolate and halved candied cherries for garnish

Blend flour with salt and sugar in a bowl. Make a well in the center; place the egg and butter in it. Stir with a fork, working from center out, to moisten flour mixture. Add wine, 1 tablespoon at a time, until dough begins to cling together. Use your hands to form dough into a ball. Cover and let stand for 15 minutes.

Roll dough out on a floured board until about 1/16-inch thick. Cut into 3½-inch circles. With rolling pin, roll circles into ovals. Wrap each oval around aluminum cannoli tubes; seal edge with egg white. Turn back ends of dough to flare slightly. Fry two or three at a time for about 1 minute or until lightly golden, in a deep saucepan with 2 inches of oil heated to 350°. Remove cannoli with tongs to drain; let cool about 5 seconds; then slip out tube, handling shell carefully. Cool shells completely; they can be stored airtight for 3 days. To serve, use a plain, large pastry tube to force ricotta filling into the cannoli pastries (fill only the number of cannoli you plan to serve at once). Sift powdered sugar over shells; garnish ends with chopped chocolate and candied cherries. Makes 25; allow at least 2 for each serving.

Ricotta filling: Whirl 2 pounds (4 cups) ricotta cheese in a covered blender until very smooth, or press through a wire strainer. Beat in 1½ cups unsifted powdered sugar and 4 teaspoons vanilla. Mix in ½ cup *each* finely chopped candied citron and candied orange peel, and ¼ cup chopped milk chocolate. Cover and chill several hours or as long as 3 days.

Fluffy ricotta filling: Follow directions for ricotta filling, preparing ½ the recipe; beat 1 cup whipping cream until stiff, then fold into ricotta.

Pistachio filling: To either of the preceding fillings, add a few drops of green food coloring to tint pale green. Use chopped blanched pistachios for garnish.

Twice Baked Cookies

These hard, crunchy cookies keep very well. Some people call them wine-dunkers, for they are frequently served with wine, to be dipped into the beverage as they are eaten.

    2 cups sugar
    1 cup (½ lb.) butter or margarine, melted
    4 tablespoons anise seed
    4 tablespoons anisette or other
       anise-flavored liqueur
    3 tablespoons whiskey, or 2 teaspoons
       vanilla and 2 tablespoons water
    2 cups coarsely chopped almonds or
       walnuts
    6 eggs
    5½ cups unsifted all-purpose flour
    1 tablespoon baking powder

Mix sugar with butter, anise seed, anise liqueur, whiskey (or vanilla and water), and nuts. Beat in the eggs. Mix flour with baking powder and stir into the sugar mixture; blend thoroughly. Cover and chill the dough for 2 to 3 hours.

Directly on greased baking sheets (without sides) shape dough with your hands to form flat loaves that are about ½ inch thick and 2 inches wide and as long as the baking sheet. Place no more than 2 loaves, parallel and well apart, on a pan. Bake in a 375° oven for 20 minutes.

Remove from oven and let loaves cool on pans until you can touch them, then cut in diagonal slices that are about ½ to ¾ inch thick. Lay slices on cut sides, close together on the baking sheets, and return to the 375° oven for 15 minutes more or until lightly toasted. Cool on wire racks and store in airtight containers. Makes about 9 dozen.

Ricotta Cheesecake

Ricotta makes this version of cheesecake less rich.

       Flavored zwieback crumbs (directions
          follow)
    3 cups (1½ lbs.) ricotta cheese
    4 eggs
    1 cup sugar
    ¼ teaspoon salt
    1 cup whipping cream
    ¼ cup unsifted all-purpose flour
    1 tablespoon grated lemon peel
    3 tablespoons lemon juice
    ¼ cup sliced almonds

Set aside ¾ cup of the flavored zwieback crumbs; reserve. Firmly press remaining crumbs in the bottom of a 9-inch cheesecake pan with removable bottom or sides. Bake in a 350° oven for about 15 minutes, or until crumbs are browned. Cool.

Whirl ricotta in a covered blender until smooth. Beat eggs to blend evenly; gradually beat in sugar until thick. Add salt, cream, and ricotta; beat well. Fold in flour, lemon peel, and juice. Pour onto cooled crust. Blend reserved crumb mixture with almonds; sprinkle evenly over top. Bake in a 350° oven for about 1 hour 10 minutes, or until cake feels firm when lightly touched near the center. Turn off oven heat and let cake cool in oven for 2 hours with door ajar. Chill; remove sides of pan. Serves 8 to 10.

Zwieback crumbs: Whirl 1 box (6 oz.) zwieback, a portion at a time, in a covered blender to make fine crumbs. Mix well with ⅓ cup sugar, ½ teaspoon ground cinnamon, and ⅓ cup melted butter.

Italian Fruit Cookies

These cookies are also baked twice.

    ½ cup (¼ lb.) butter or margarine
    2 cups sugar
    1½ teaspoons anise extract
    6 eggs
    5 cups unsifted all-purpose flour
    1 tablespoon baking powder
    ½ teaspoon salt
    1⅓ cups diced mixed candied fruit, candied
       citron, or ⅔ cup candied fruit and ⅔
       cup whole pine nuts (pignoli)

Cream butter and sugar in a large bowl. Blend in anise extract and eggs. Mix together the flour, baking powder, and salt; gradually mix into butter and egg mixture. Chill dough 1 hour. Divide dough into four equal parts.

Taking one portion of dough at a time, roll out on a floured board to make a rectangle 12 inches long and 8 inches wide. Sprinkle surface of dough evenly with ⅓ cup of the candied fruit or nuts. Starting with the wide side of the rectangle, roll dough tightly to make a long, compact loaf. Place rolls on lightly greased baking sheets (2 loaves to a baking sheet). Bake in 375° oven for 25 to 30 minutes, until lightly browned.

Remove from oven; let cool on pans for 5 minutes; cut in diagonal slices, ½ inch thick. Lay slices, cut side down, close together on the baking sheets and return to the 375° oven for 16 to 18 minutes, until lightly toasted. Cool on racks and store in airtight containers or freeze. Makes about 6 dozen.

Almond Macaroons

Instead of the more usual canned almond paste, these tasty macaroons start with whole almonds. We think you'll find the flavor worth the effort.

1½ cups blanched almonds
1½ cups sugar
¼ teaspoon salt
¾ teaspoon almond extract
6 tablespoons egg white (about 3 egg whites; beat lightly with a fork before measuring)
All-purpose flour, if needed
Whole blanched almonds or whole pine nuts (pignoli)

Reduce the 1½ cups nuts to a coarse meal or flour-like consistency by one of these methods: whirl about ½ cup nuts at a time in a blender; pass through the fine blade of a food chopper; or grate nuts on a nut grater, using the finest surface.

Combine the nuts in a bowl with sugar, salt, and almond extract, and mix well.

Beat egg whites with nuts with an electric mixer or by hand until the mixture holds together in a firm, slightly shiny mass; takes about 5 minutes. The mixture should not flow.

Test bake one cooky: measure out 1 tablespoon of the dough and shape it into a ball, flatten slightly onto a greased and flour-dusted baking sheet, and bake in a 350° oven.

Within 10 minutes you can tell if the cooky will hold its shape. The ball will spread and flatten slightly but should keep its round shape. If it spreads out thinly, add 2 tablespoons of all-purpose flour to the dough, mixing very well.

Test bake another cooky if necessary; continue adding flour 2 tablespoons at a time and test baking until dough has the desired consistency (one or two tests will usually be adequate). Then shape the balance of the dough on greased and flour-dusted baking sheets.

Either make scant 1-tablespoon-size mounds by forcing dough through a pastry bag without a tip (you will have to disengage the dough with your fingertips), or form the dough in scant 1-tablespoon-size balls and flatten slightly onto baking sheets. Top each cooky with an almond or scatter with pine nuts, if you like.

Bake in a 350° oven for 18 to 25 minutes, or until lightly browned. Remove immediately from the pans with a spatula and cool on wire racks; handle the cookies carefully, for they will be soft and crush easily.

When cool and crisp, store the macaroons in airtight containers or freeze them. Makes about 30 cookies, each about 2 inches in diameter.

Cialde

Traditionally made for the holiday season, cialde and pizelle are thin, crisp cookies baked in special irons (see page 5).

You can make each cooky in either of the decorative cialde or pizelle irons, or you can bake them in the Scandinavian wafer iron used for krum krager.

1 cup sugar
1 egg
2 teaspoons vanilla
2 tablespoons each whiskey and salad oil
⅔ cup milk
1 tablespoon anise seed
1½ cups unsifted all-purpose flour
Salad oil

Beat to blend the sugar, egg, vanilla, whiskey, the 2 tablespoons salad oil, and milk. Stir in smoothly the anise seed and flour. Place the cialde cooky iron (about 5 inch diameter) directly over moderate heat until iron is hot enough (turn over occasionally to heat evenly) to make a drop of water sizzle and dance when it hits the open iron. Brush the inside of the iron lightly with salad oil. Put a small spoonful of batter in the center of one side of the iron and close. After about 10 seconds, clamp shut or squeeze handles tightly to completely flatten cooky (if some batter oozes out, scrape from edge of iron; you'll soon learn to judge the exact amount you need). Cook, turning frequently until cooky is a pale gold; takes about ½ minute. Open iron slightly to check progress during the baking. Shift iron about on heat if one edge seems to cook more quickly than another. Carefully open iron and lift out cialde. Roll immediately into a cylinder; they become too crisp to roll if allowed to cool. Repeat to make each cooky. Let cool completely, then store airtight. Makes 30 cookies, each about 5 inches in diameter.

Ossa da Mordere

Another favorite Italian cooky is this rather hard, pale cooky, appropriately named "bones to chew" and intended for dunking in tea, wine, or strong coffee.

3 egg whites
1¾ cups sugar
½ teaspoon grated lemon peel
½ teaspoon baking powder
1½ cups very coarsely chopped blanched almonds
1¾ cups unsifted all-purpose flour

With an electric mixer, beat whites and sugar with lemon peel and baking powder until smoothly blended. With a heavy spoon, work the nuts in thoroughly, then the flour.

Lightly flour your hands, then pinch off tablespoon-size lumps of dough and shape like short sturdy bones. Place cookies slightly apart on a greased baking sheet and bake in a 375° oven for 10 to 12 minutes or until pale brown. Cool on wire racks; store airtight. Makes about 3½ dozen.

Fave dei Morti

These "beans of the dead" cookies resemble "bones to chew," but the ground nuts make them richer.

1¼ cups whole unblanched almonds
⅔ cup pine nuts (pignoli)
1¼ cups sugar
½ teaspoon baking powder
¼ cup unsifted all-purpose flour
2 egg whites

Whirl nuts, a few at a time, in a covered blender, until they have a flour-like consistency. In a bowl, mix the nuts with the sugar, baking powder, and flour. Stir in the egg whites with a heavy spoon, mixing until dough sticks together.

Shape in 1-teaspoon-size balls and flatten slightly on a greased baking sheet; do not allow cookies to touch. With a teaspoon handle, press in one edge of the cooky round to make a bean-like indentation.

Bake in a 375° oven for 10 to 12 minutes or until pale brown. Cool on wire racks; store airtight. Makes about 5½ dozen.

Pizelle

The pizelle iron is characterized by its rippled surface. The cookies hold the imprinted pattern of the iron as they cool but not much of the rippled form.

2 eggs
6 tablespoons sugar
¼ cup salad oil
2 teaspoons vanilla
1 teaspoon grated lemon peel
1 cup unsifted all-purpose flour

Beat together until smoothly blended the eggs, sugar, oil, vanilla, lemon peel, and flour. Place fluted 5-inch diameter pizelle cooky iron over moderate heat and heat as directed for Cialde iron (left). Do not brush iron with oil; put 1 rounded tablespoon batter in

the center of the iron, close, and cook, turning frequently until cooky is golden. Lift from iron at once and place flat on wire racks to cool. Repeat to make each cooky; store airtight. Makes about 14 cookies, each about 5 inches in diameter.

Florentines

As one of Italy's first fancy pastries, these confection-like cookies date back to the 15th or 16th century, and most likely came from Florence, as their name implies. Chances are the Medicis and other Italian families of this period knew these cookies well.

1 cup sliced almonds
¼ cup whipping cream
⅓ cup sugar
¼ cup (⅛ lb.) butter or margarine
½ cup candied orange peel, finely chopped
2 tablespoons all-purpose flour
¼ pound semisweet chocolate

Whirl ½ cup of the sliced almonds in a blender or put through a nut grater to grind finely. Combine cream, sugar, and butter in a pan. Cook, stirring occasionally, over low heat until butter is melted. Turn heat to medium high and bring mixture to boil. Remove mixture from the heat. Stir in sliced almonds, ground almonds, orange peel, and flour.

Drop by level tablespoonfuls on lightly greased, floured baking sheets (allow 6 cookies to each 12 by 15-inch pan). Flatten with back of a spoon to about 2 inches in diameter. Bake in a 350° oven for 10 to 12 minutes, or until the edges are slightly browned (centers will still be bubbling when you remove them from the oven). Let cool for 1 or 2 minutes. Carefully transfer each cooky from the baking sheet to a wire rack. Cool, then turn cookies upside down on a piece of waxed paper.

Melt the chocolate over hot (not boiling) water. Using a brush, paint a thin layer of chocolate over the back of each cooky. Let cool several hours until the chocolate has hardened. Store cookies in a covered container in refrigerator up to 2 weeks, or freeze for longer storage. Makes about 15 large cookies.

Glossary

This glossary will help you to pronounce the Italian words in this book (plus a few French ones that crept across the border).

al	ahl
all'	ahl
alla	*ahl* lah
amor	ah *more*
antipasti	ahn tee *pahs* tee
antipasto	ahn tee *pahs* toe
Asiago	ah see *ah* go
baccalá	bah kah *lah*
bagna	*bahn* yah
basilíco	bah *see* lee koh
bécco	*beck* koh
bel	bell
biroldo	bee *rol* doe
blanc	blahnk
bollito	bol *lee* toh
brodo	*broh* doe
buccellati	boo chel *lah* tee
buco	boo koh
caffé	kahf *feh*
calzone	kal *zoe* neh
Campari	kam *pah* ree
cannelini	kahn neh *lee* nee
cannelloni	kahn nel *low* nee
cannoli	kahn *noh* lee
capellini	kap ell *lee* nee
caponata	kah poh *nah* tah
cappuccino	kap pooch *cee* noh
carbonara	kar boh *nahr* ah
carciofi	kar chee *off* fee
cassata	kah *sah* tah
Castiglioni	kas tell *own* nee
cauda	*kow* dah
Cavour	*kah* vor
Cellini	cheel *lee* nee
cialde	chee *all* dey
ciocca	chee *ouk* kah
cioppino	chee oh *pee* noh
cipolle	chee *pole* leh
colomba	kol *om* bah
con	kone
conchighe	kohn *see* geeh
coppa	*koh* pah
coteghino	koh tee *gee* noh
cotto	*koht* toh
cresto	*kress* toh
crostini	kros *tee* nee
cruda	*krew* dah
da	dah
dei	dey
dente	*den* teh
di	dee
ditali	dee *tah* lee
ditalini	dee tah *lee* nee
dolce	*dol* chay

e	eh
espresso	es *press* soh
fagiolini	fah gee oh *lee* nee
farfalle	far *fall* leh
fave	*fah* veh
fettuce	fet *too* cheh
fettucini	fet too *chee* nee
finanziera	fee nan zee *er* ah
fiorentina	fee or en *tee* dah
focaccia	fo *kah* chee ah
fonduta	fon *doo* tah
fontina	fon *tee* nah
forno	*for* noh
forte	*for* teh
frisio	frees ee oh
frittata	free *tah* tah
fritto	*free* toh
fusilli	fuh *seal* lee
galantina	gal an *tee* nah
gallo	*gall* loh
gateau	gah *toe*
Genovese	jen oh *vay* seh
giardiniera	jar dee *nyear* ah
gnocchi	*nyok* kee
gorgonzola	gor guhn *tzoh* lah
grande	*grahn* deh
grandine	grahn *dee* neh
grissini	gree *see* nee
Honoré	ahn noh *rey*
indorato	en doh *rah* toh
Inglese	ing *lay* seh
insalata	en sah *lah* tah
Julio	*jewel* ee oh
la	lah
lasagne	lah *sah* neh
latte	*lah* teh
lingua	*ling* wah
linguine	ling *wee* neh
macchinetta	mah kee *net* tah
manicotti	mahn nee *kot* tee
mare	*mah* reh
marengo	mah *rang* oh
marinara	mahr een *ah* rah
Marino	mahr *een* oh
maritata	mar ee *tah* tah
Marsala	mar *sah* lah
mascarpone	mas kar *pone* ney
Medici	*meh* dee chee
melanzane	mel ahn *zah* neh
Milanese	meal ahn *eh* seh
minestra	mee *nes* trah
minestrone	mee nes *troh* neh
misto	*mee* stoh
mordere	*more* der reh
morselata	more seh *lah* tah
mortadella	mor tah *del* lah
morti	*more* tee
mozzarella	motz zar *el* ah
ossa	*oh* sah
osso	*oh* soh
paese	pah *eh* seh
pane	*pah* neh
pandoro	pahn *door* oh
panettone	pahn et *toe* neh

panforte	pahn *for* teh
Parmigiáno	par mee *jon* oh
Parmesan	par meh *sahn*
Pasqua	*pas* qwah
pasta	*pahs* tah
patate	pah *tah* teh
pavese	pah *vez* eh
pecorino	peck oh *ree* noh
peperoncini	per per ohn *chee* nee
pesto	*pest* oh
picatte	pee *kaht* teh
pignoli	peen *yoh* lee
pinzimonio	peen see mohn ee oh
pizza	*pee* zah
pizzelle	pee *zel* leh
polenta	poe *len* tah
pollo	*pole* loh
prosciutto	proh *shoot* toe
provolone	proh voh *loh* neh
ramerino	rahm er ee noh
Rapallo	rah *pahl* loh
ravioli	rah vee *oh* lee
raviolini	rah vee oh *lee* nee
ricotta	ree *kot* tah
rigate	ree *gah* teh
rigatoni	ree gah *toe* nee
risotto	ree *soht* toe
Roma	*rohm* ah
Romano	roh *mah* noh
rustica	*roos* tee kah
salame	sah *lah* meh
salami	sah *lah* mee
salsa	*sahl* sah
salsiccia	sahl *see* chee ah
saltimbocca	sal teem *boh* kah
san	sahn
Scala	*skah* lah
scallopini	skahl loh *pee* nee
scoglio	*skohl* ee oh
Siena	see *en* ah
spaghetti	spah *get* tee
spumone	spoo *moe* neh
St.	sahnt
stracciatella	strah chee ah *tel* lah
tagliarini	tahl yah *ree* nee
tagliatelle	tah yah *tell* leh
tonnato	tohn *nah* toe
torrone	tor *roh* neh
torta	*tor* tah
tortellini	tor tel *lee* nee
tortoni	tor *toe* nee
Toscano	toe *scah* noh
trippa	*tree* pah
umidi	*oo* mee dee
uovo	*woe* voh
verde	*vehr* deh
vermicelli	vehr mee *cheel* lee
Verona	vehr *oh* nah
vin	veen
vitello	vee *tahl* loh
zabaglione	zah bah *yoh* neh
zampino	zam *pee* noh
zucchini	zoo *key* nee
zuppa	*zoo* pah

Index